Kingston Ontario Book 1 in Colour Photos, Saving Our History One Photo at a Time

Photography
by Barbara Raué
2016

Series Name:
Cruising Ontario

Book 140: Kingston Book 1

Cover photo: 294 King Street East – Custom House, Page 12

Series Name: Cruising Ontario
Saving Our History One Photo at a Time
in colour photos

Books Available in Alphabetical Order:
Aberfoyle, Acton, Alton, Ancaster, Arthur, Aylmer, Ayr, Bloomingdale, Brantford, Burlington, Caledon, Caledonia, Cambridge, Clifford, Conestogo, Delhi, Dorchester to Aylmer, Drayton, Drumbo, Dundas, Eden Mills, Elmira, Elora, Fergus, Guelph, Hagersville, Hamilton, Hanover, Harriston, Hespeler, Jarvis, Kitchener, Linwood, Listowel, London, Lucknow, Mono, Mount Forest, Neustadt, New Hamburg, Niagara-on-the-Lake, Oakville, Orangeville, Orillia, Owen Sound, Palmerston, Peterborough, Port Elgin, Preston, Rockwood, Seaforth, Sheffield, Shelburne, Simcoe, Southampton, St. Jacobs, St. Thomas, Stoney Creek, Stratford, Tillsonburg, Waterdown, Waterford, Waterloo, Wellesley, Wingham

Book 114-116: Waterloo
Book 117-119: Windsor
Book 120: Amherstburg
Book 122: Essex
Book 123-124: Kingsville
Book 125-127: Woodstock
Book 128: Thamesford
Book 129: St. Mary's
Book 133-136: Sarnia
Book 137: Petrolia
Book 138-139: Welland
Book 140-145: Kingston

Other Books by Barbara Raue

Coins of Gold

Arrows, Indians and Love

The Life and Times of Barbara
Volume 1: Inventions That Have Enhanced My Life
Volume 2: Entertainment That I Have Enjoyed
Volume 3: East Coast Trips
Volume 4: Olympics Have Always Intrigued Me
Volume 5: Wonders of the World
Volume 6: Caribbean Cruises We Have Enjoyed
Volume 7: Animals
Volume 8: Storms and Other Major Disasters in My Lifetime
Volume 9: Wars, Terrorist Attacks and Major Disasters

The Cromwell Family Book

Laura Secord Discovered

Daddy Where Are You?

Visit Barbara's website to view all of her books
http://barbararaue.ca

Table of Contents

In October 1783, at Carleton Island, Captain William Redford Carleton of the King's Royal Regiment of New York, met with the local Mississauga Indians led by the elderly Mynass. Crawford, acting for the British government, purchased from the Mississaugas for some clothing, ammunition and colored cloth, a large tract of land east of the Bay of Quinte. In September 1783, Deputy Surveyor-General John Collins was despatched to Cataraqui by Governor Haldimand to lay out townships for Loyalist settlers. By the end of the year, the front concessions of four townships stretching from Cataraqui to the Bay of Quinte had been surveyed. A fifth township was laid out the following summer. The land was subsequently settled by United Empire Loyalists and Britain's allies who had been forced to leave their homes in the new United States.

Earl Street has a wide range of homes, some originally built for factory workers and others for the wealthy. They include a variety of frame, stone, stone and brick, and all-brick homes. They have different rooflines, porches, trim, chimneys, windows and transoms.

The Kingston Custom House was built 1856-59 for the government of the united Canadas. The symmetrical composition of the two-storey ashlar building, surmounted by a restrained cornice and parapet, draws on the British classical tradition. The orderly design is achieved through repeated use of semi-circular forms for doors and windows. The Custom House and the nearby Post Office are fine examples of the architectural quality of mid-nineteenth century administrative buildings. See Page 12.

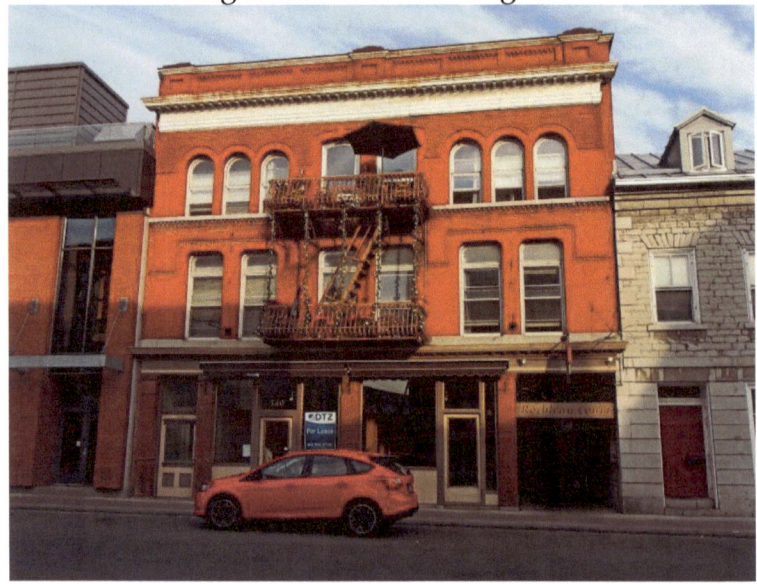

340 King Street East – dentil moulding, cornice brackets, voussoirs

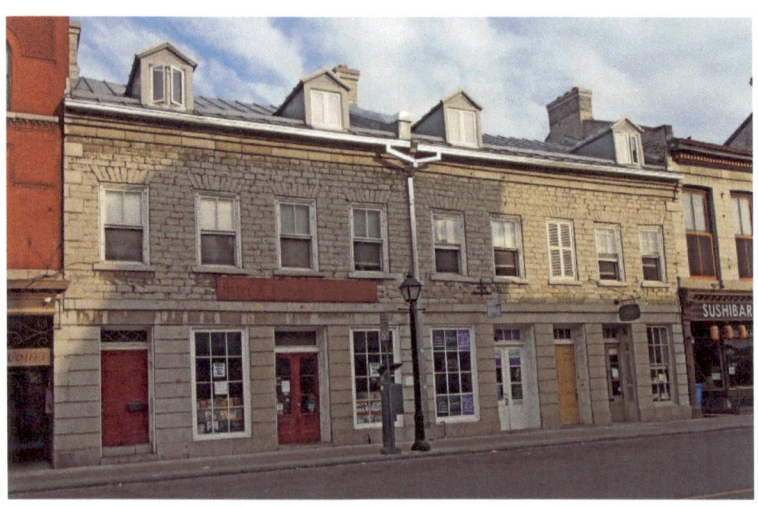

348 King Street East – limestone, two storeys, dormers

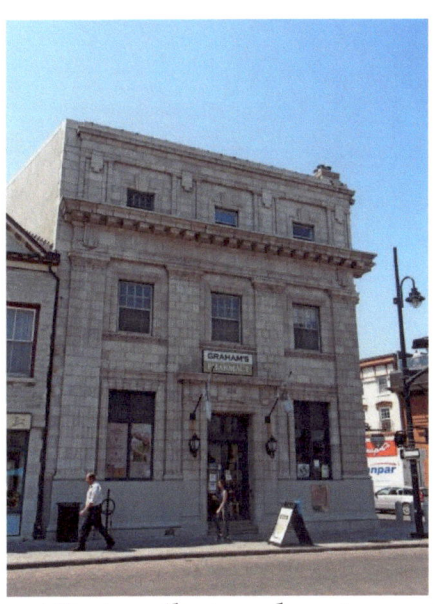

328 King Street East – pilasters, keystones above upper windows

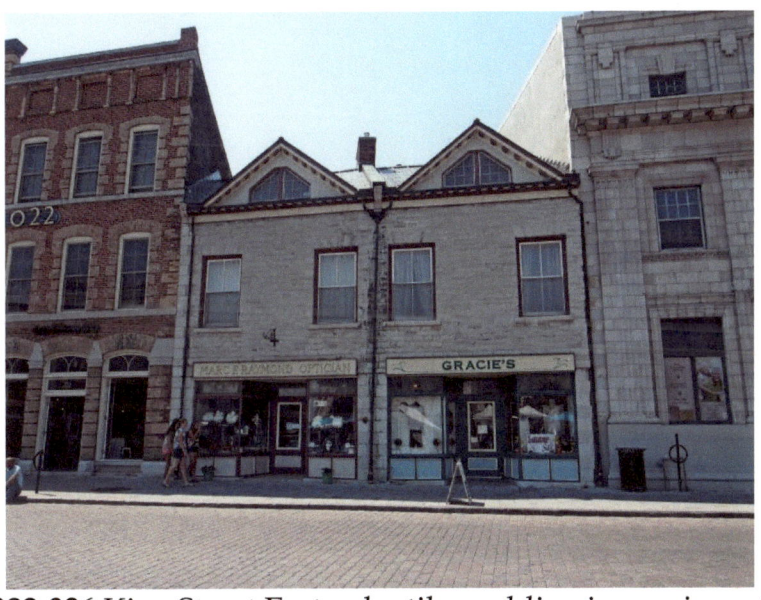

322-326 King Street East – dentil moulding in cornices of gables and below gables; 322 has dichromatic brickwork and corner quoins

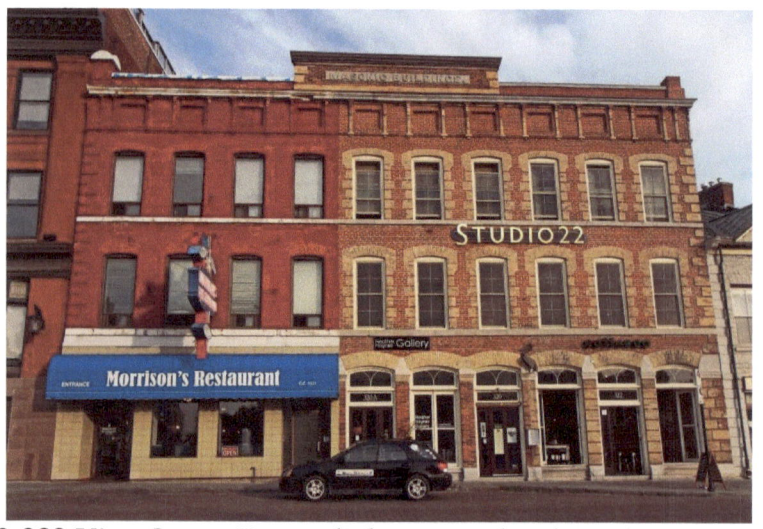

320-322 King Street East – dichromatic brickwork, voussoirs, quoining

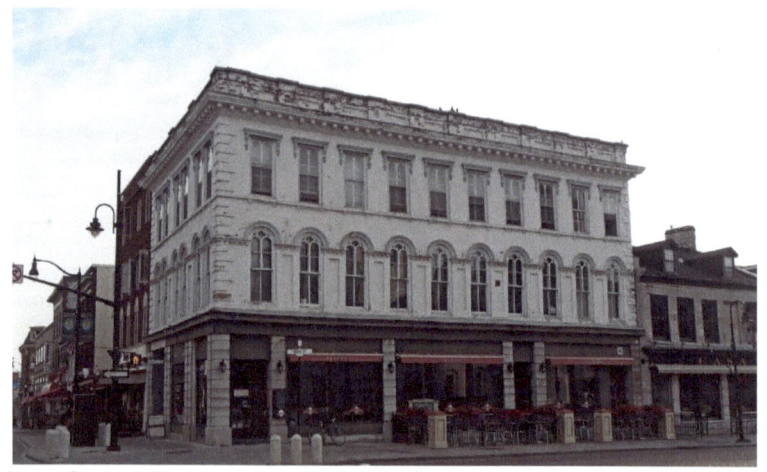

King Street East, corner of Brock Street – cornice brackets, window drip moulds, dentil moulding

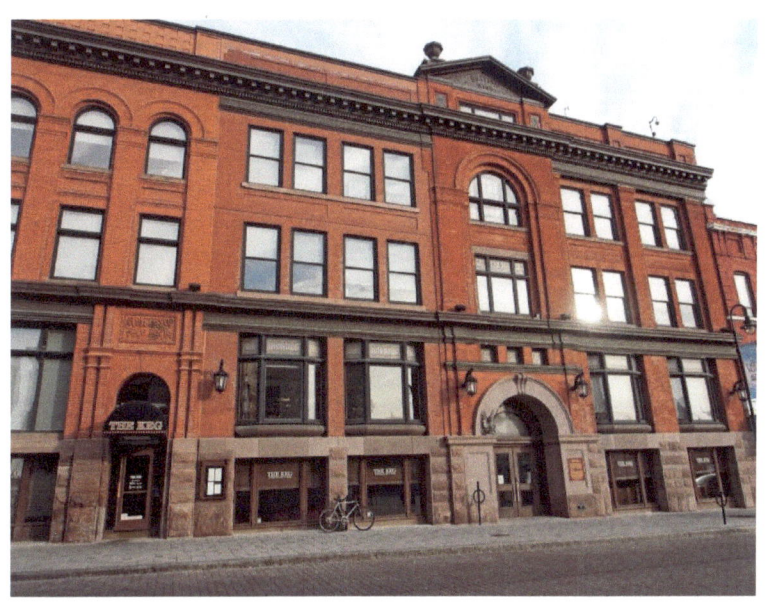

310 King Street East – dentil moulding, pediment
– British Whig Building - 1895

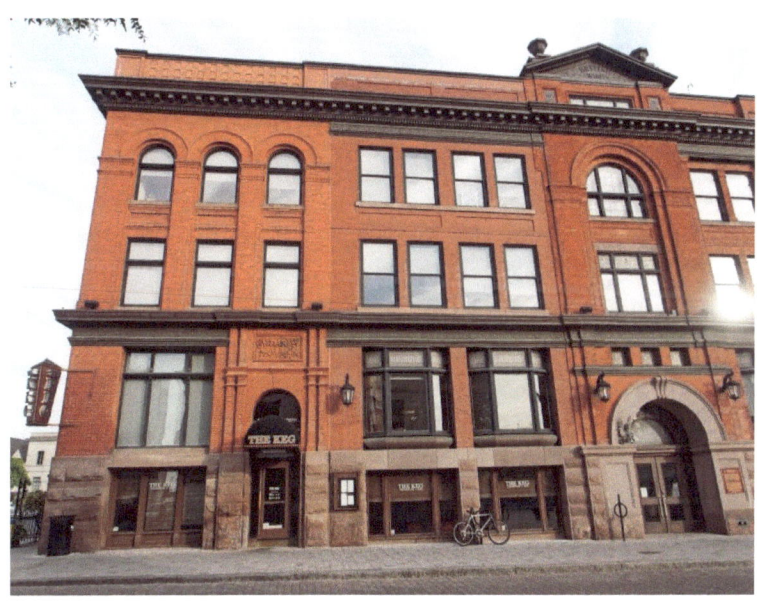

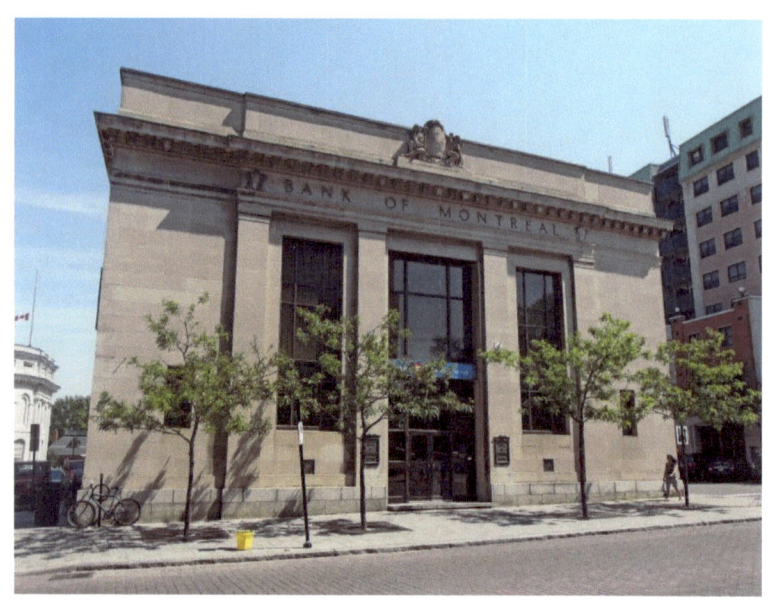

297 King Street East – Bank of Montreal – established 1917 – pilasters, cornice brackets

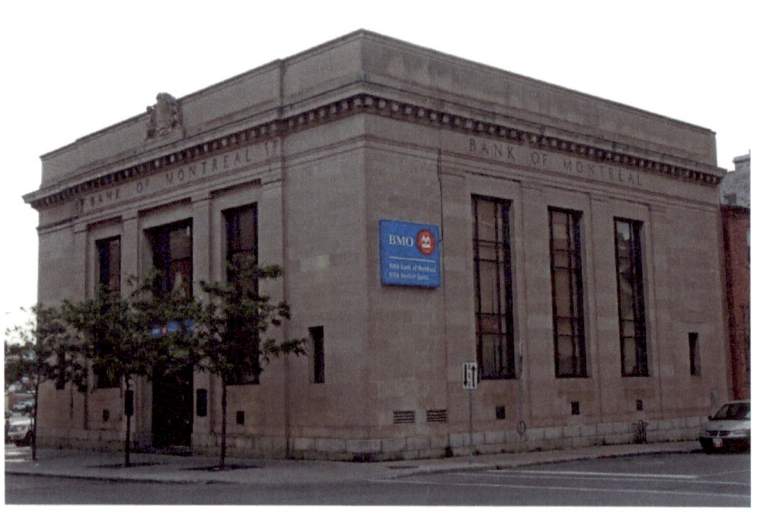

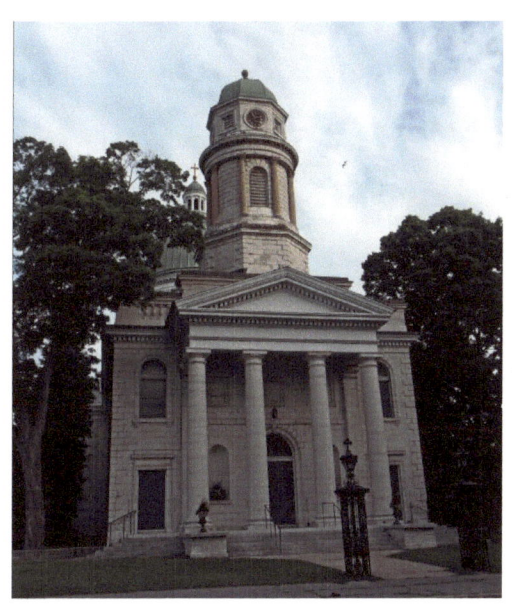

270 King Street East – St. George's Anglican Cathedral - 1825
– Classical style – Tuscan porticos

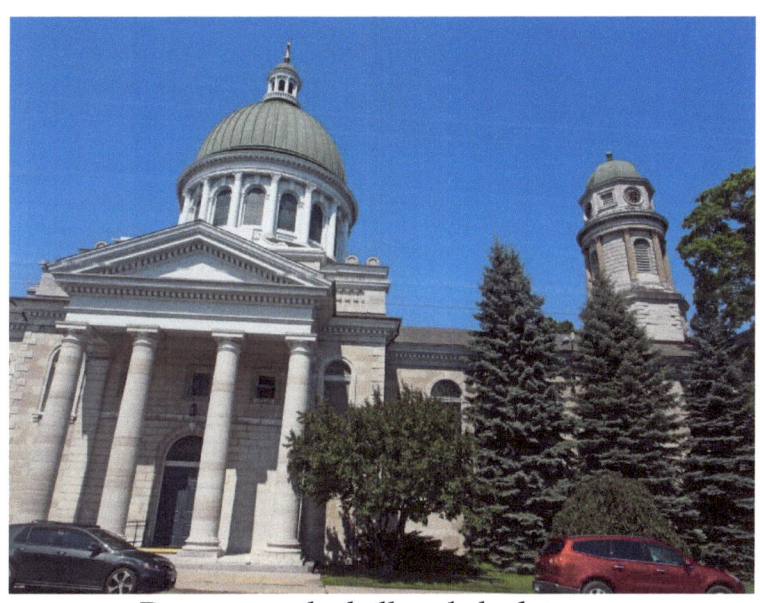

Dome, cupola, bell and clock tower

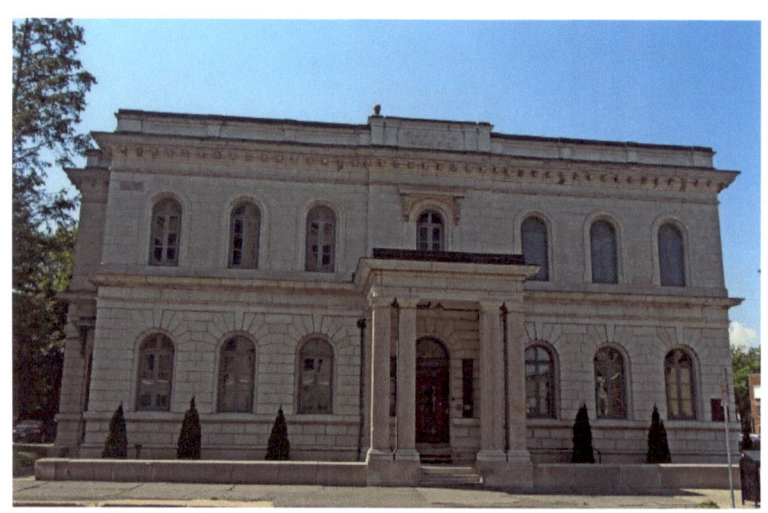

294 King Street East – Custom House – 1856-1858 - Classical Revival style made from hammered limestone blocks from local quarries – voussoirs on lower windows and door, pillared entrance, window hood on second floor centre window

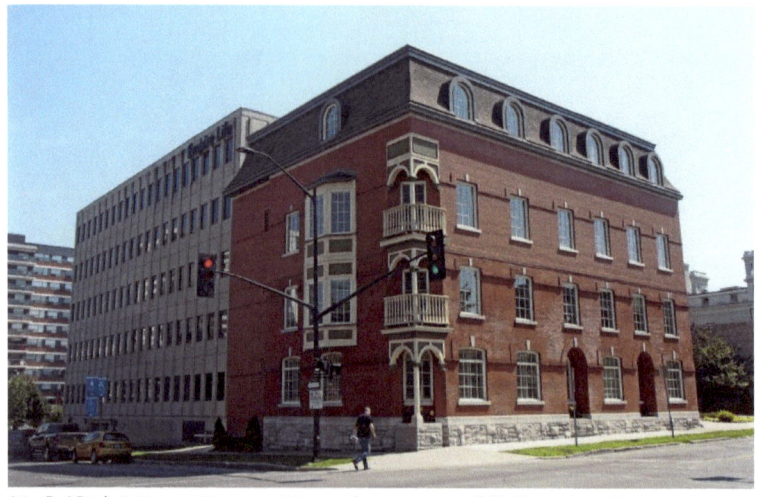

261-263½ King Street East (corner of Johnson Street) – red brick building built in 1904 as three townhouses; bottom floors were later commercial; it underwent a prize-winning reconstruction after a fire in 2005; another storey was added at this time – now part of the Empire Life complex

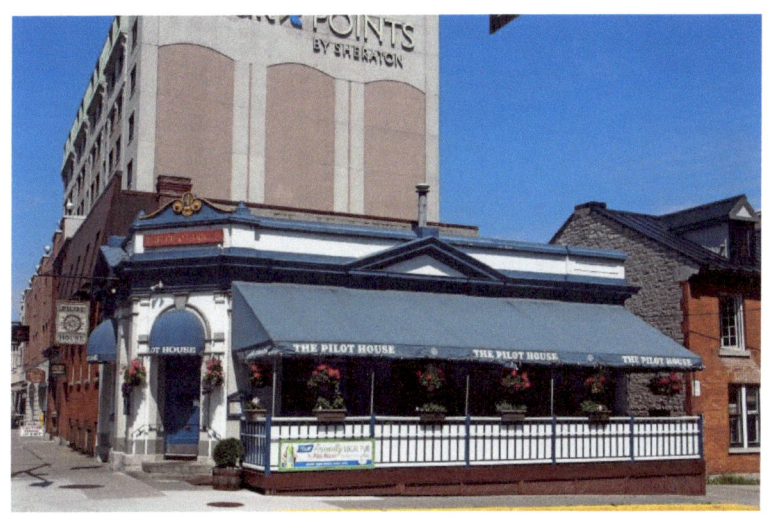

265 King Street East – The Pilot House

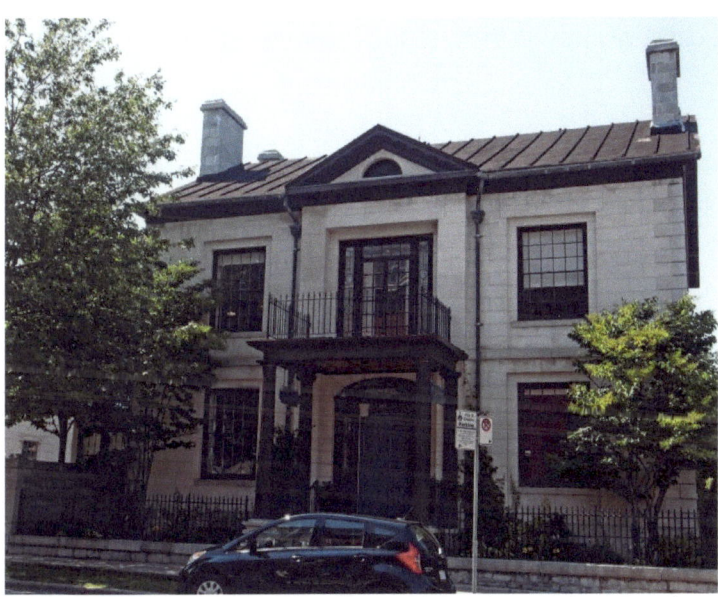

264 King Street East – Gildersleeve House – 1825 – Neoclassical
style limestone house now covered with stucco grooved to simulate
dressed stone. Henry and Sarah Gildersleeve came from
Connecticut after the War of 1812; he launched the first steamboat
on the Great Lakes, the Frontenac, in 1816.

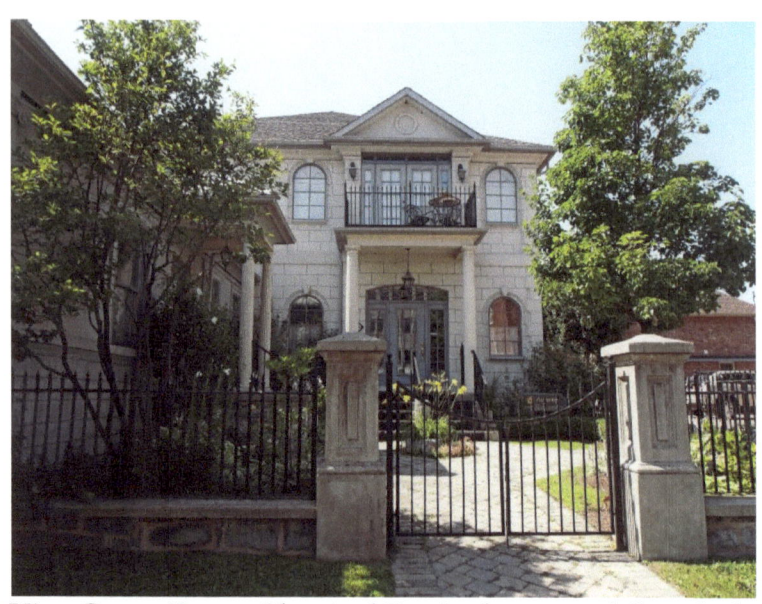

258 King Street East – Classical Revival – second floor balcony, pediment, keystones, sidelights and transom window

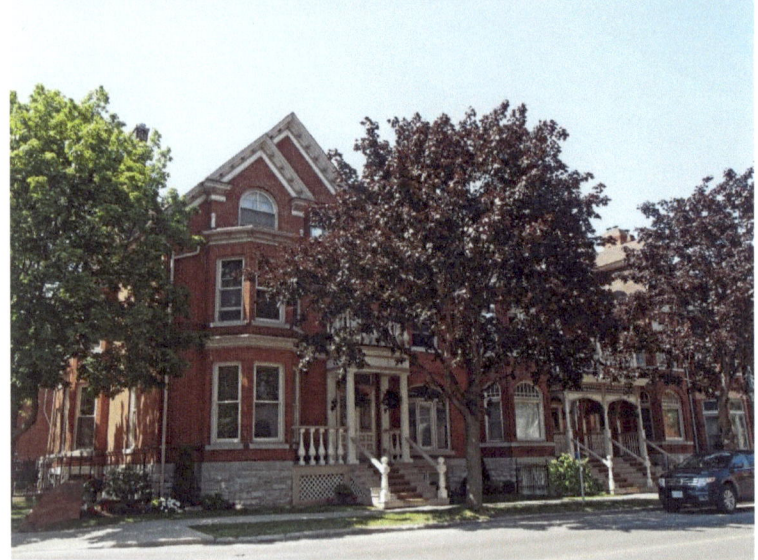

244 King Street East townhouses – 1890 brick – double-gabled roof – one gable over the two-storey bay windows, and a larger one over the windows and entranceway

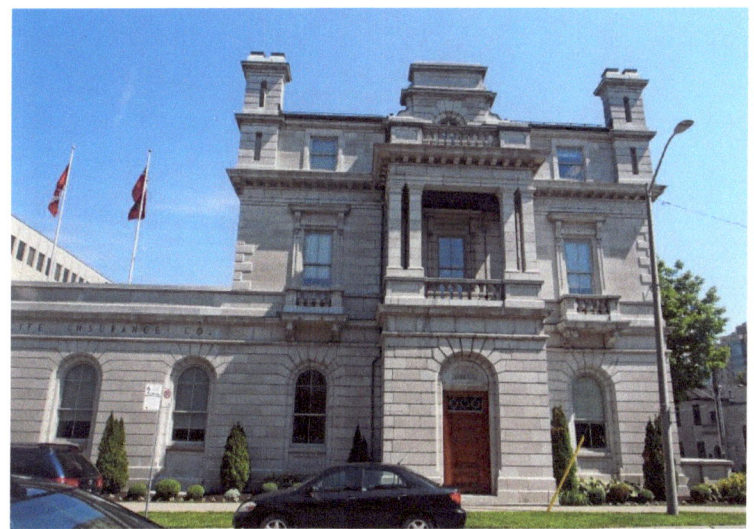

243 King Street East – Renaissance Revival designed in 1853 for Commercial Bank of the Midland District – now head office of Empire Life Insurance – three-storeys, smooth ashlar stone with different treatments to give it variety and grandeur

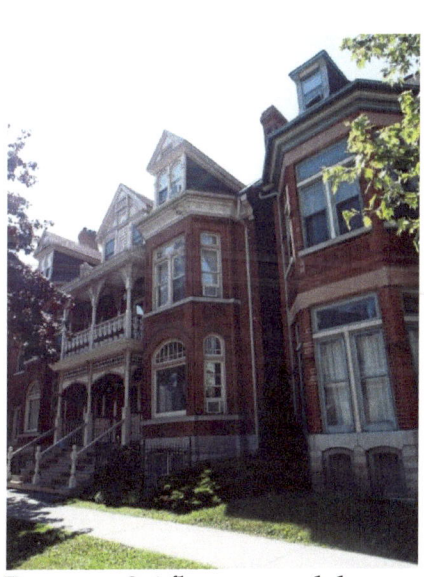

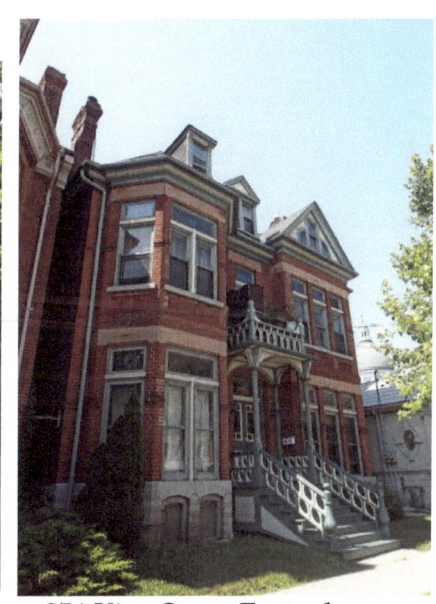

Dormers, 2nd floor verandah

254 King Street East - dormers

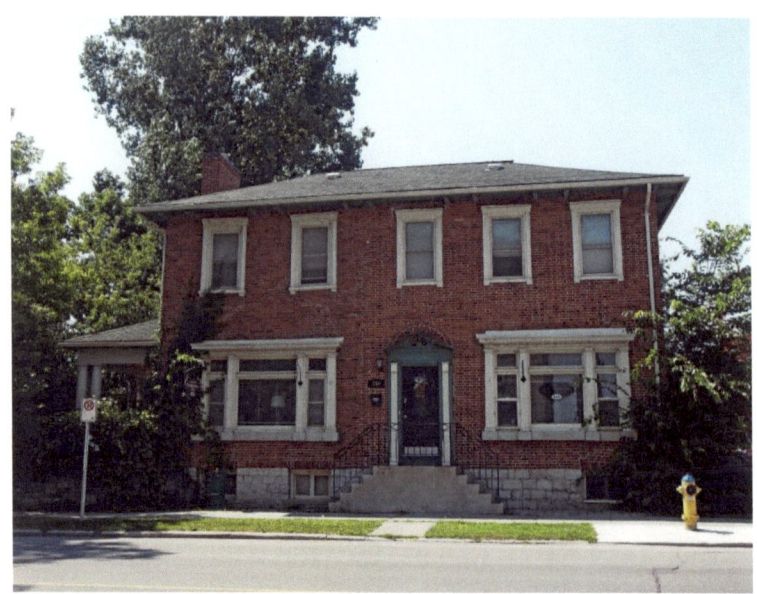

240 King Street East – Summer House Inn established 1829
– Victorian style - hipped roof, two-storey, red brick

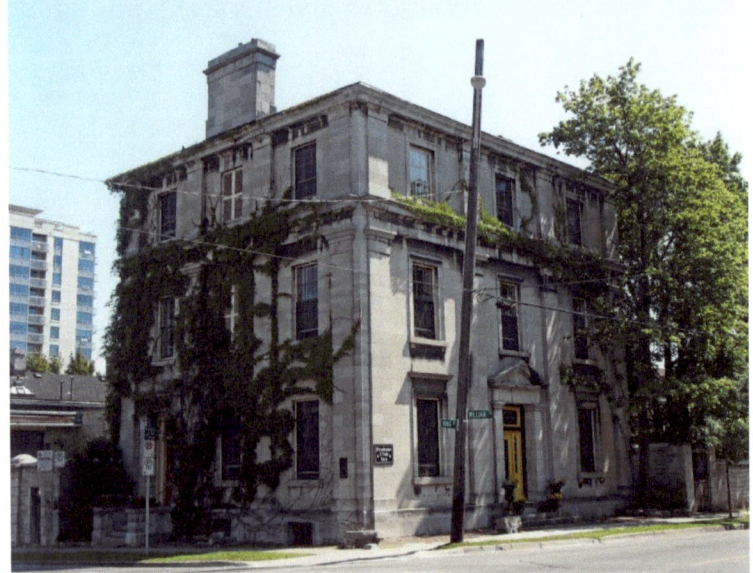

225 King Street East – 1845-46 – designed as a bank in Classical Revival style – The Bank of Montreal used it until 1906; it became a men's club; since 2000 it has operated as Frontenac Club Inn – symmetrical and elaborate windows

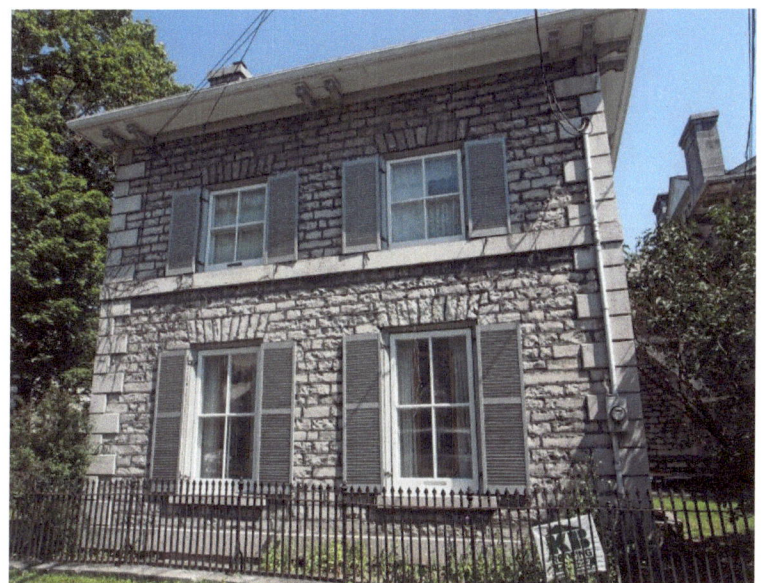

King Street East – stone building, corner quoins

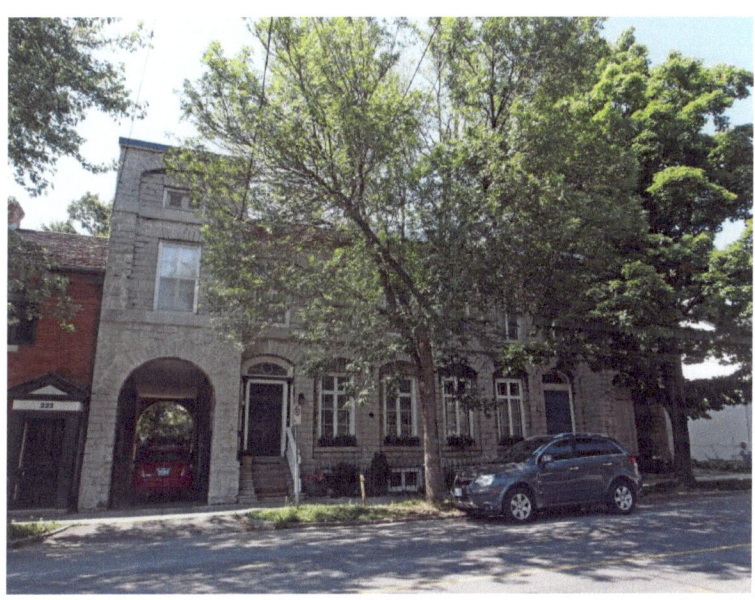

224-228 King Street East - 1843 - two storey stone double
house with a carriageway at each end

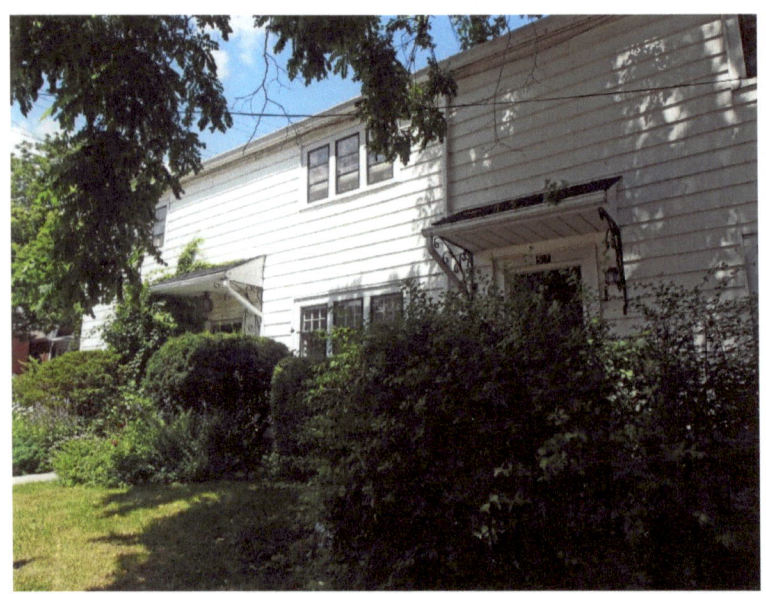

57-59 Gore Street (corner of King Street East) – wooden house is one of the oldest buildings in Kingston, part of it having been built about 1808

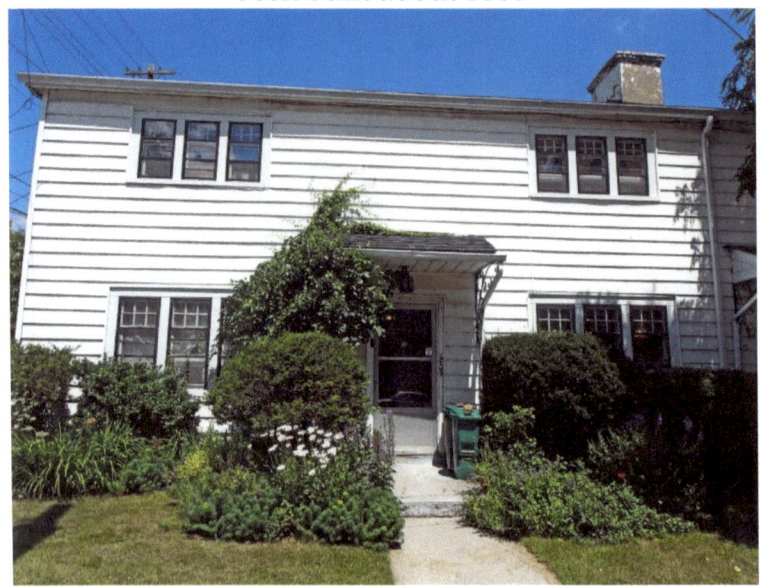

59 Gore Street

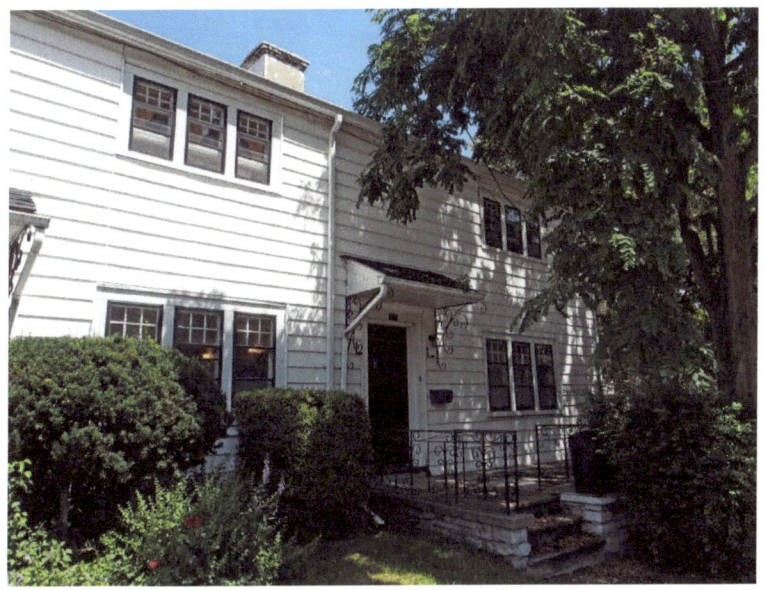

57 Gore Street

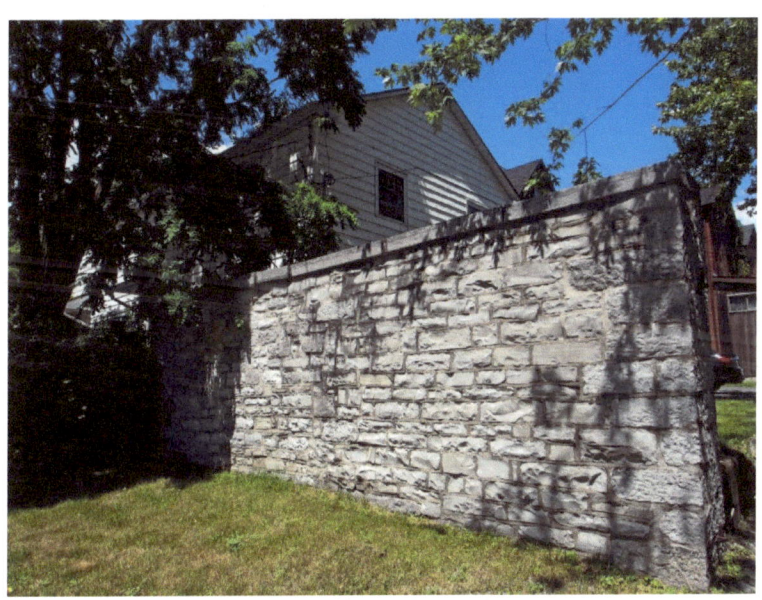

Stone wall on Gore Street

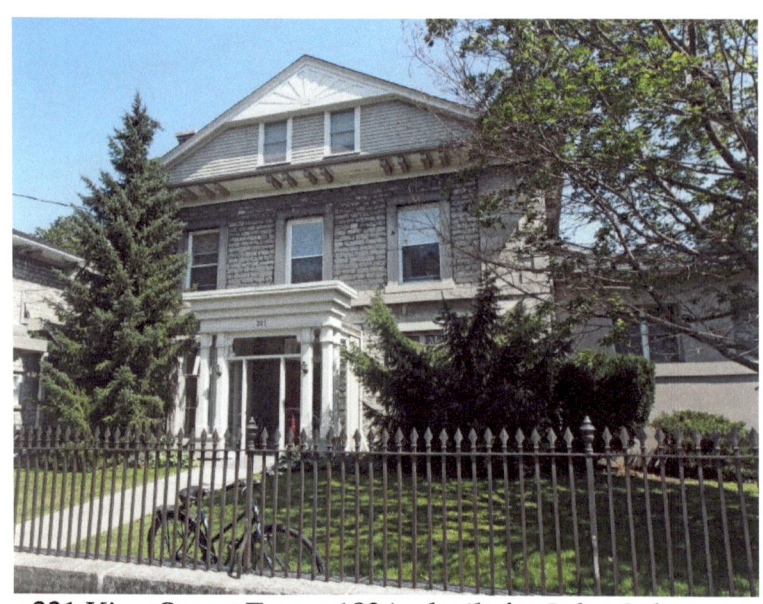

221 King Street East – 1834 – built for John Solomon Cartwright and his wife Sarah; John was a lawyer, judge, banker and member of the Legislative Assembly of Upper Canada

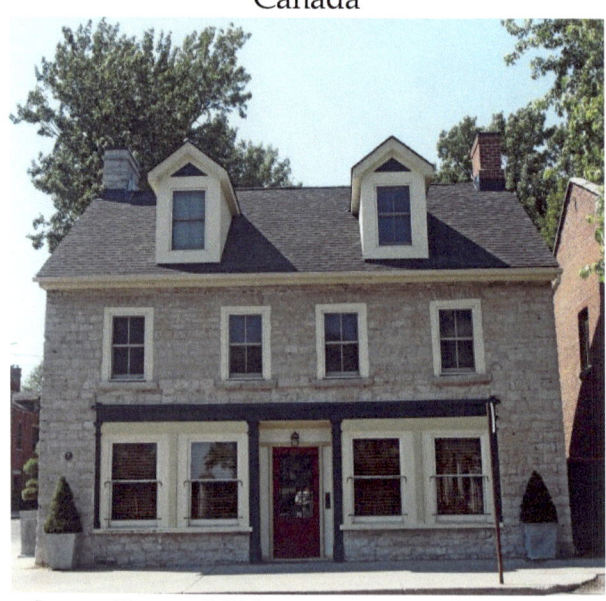

218 King Street East – 1833 – two-storey limestone, dormers

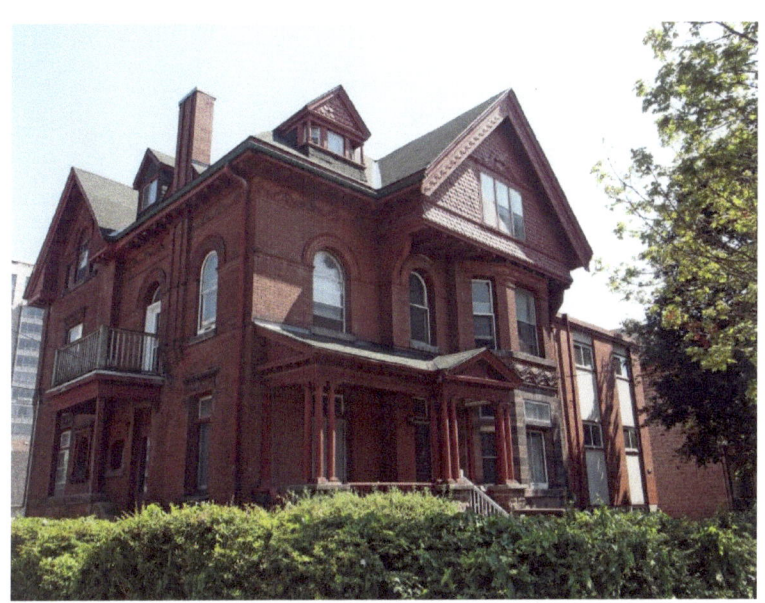

213 King Street East – Italianate – decorative brickwork below cornice and above first floor windows, dormers with fish scale pattern in the gables, pediment, columns with Ionic capitals supporting the verandah

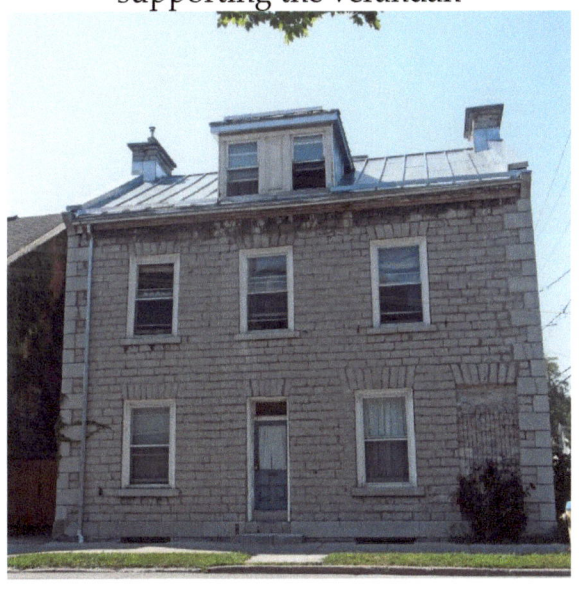

212 King Street East – two storeys, dormer in attic, corner quoins

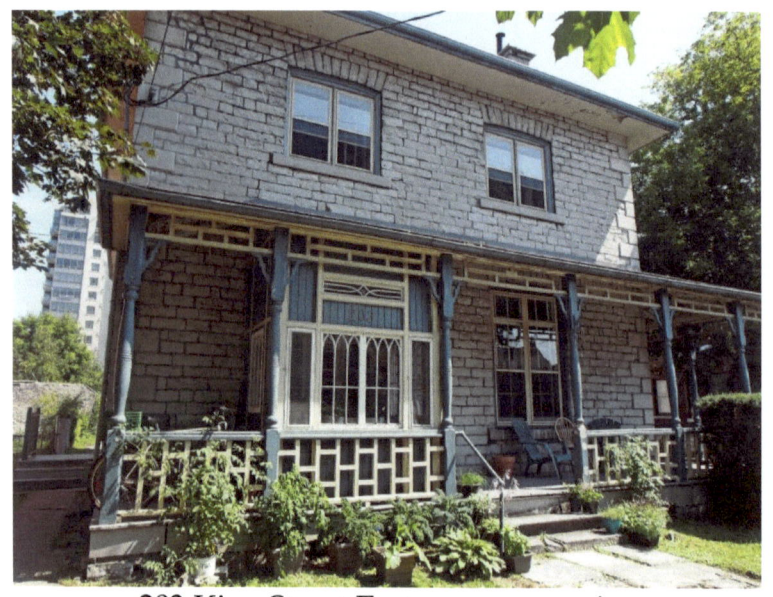

203 King Street East – corner quoins

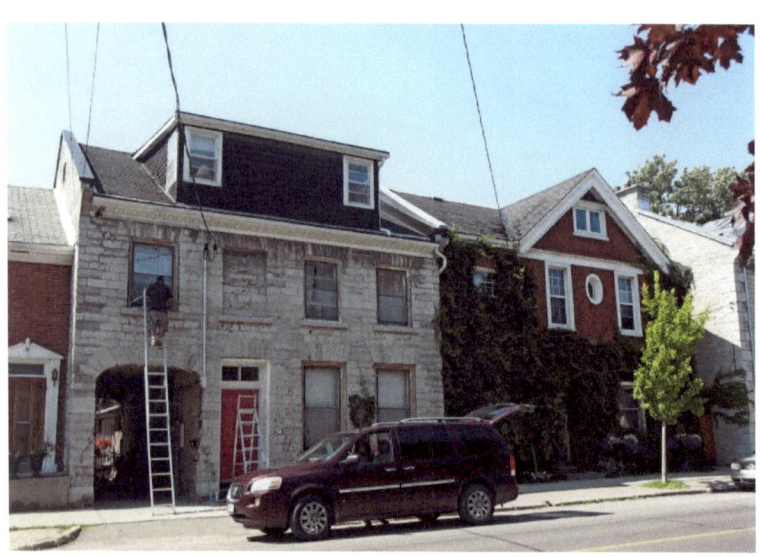

204 King Street East – shed dormer in attic

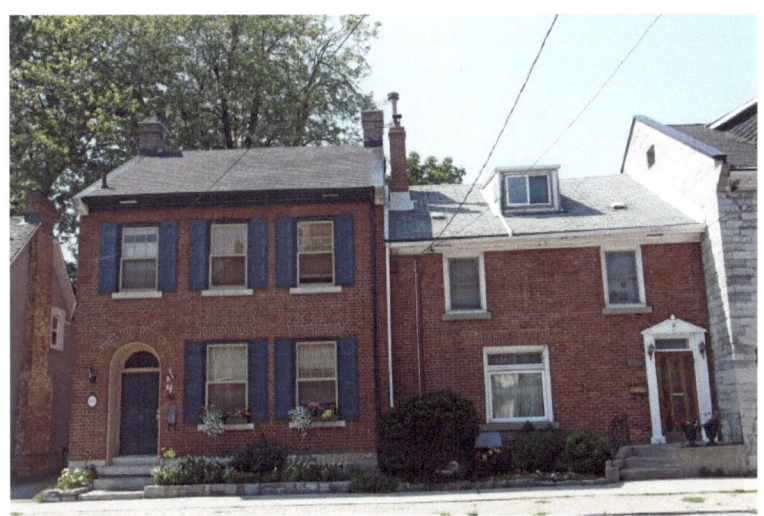

198-202 King Street East – voussoirs above door

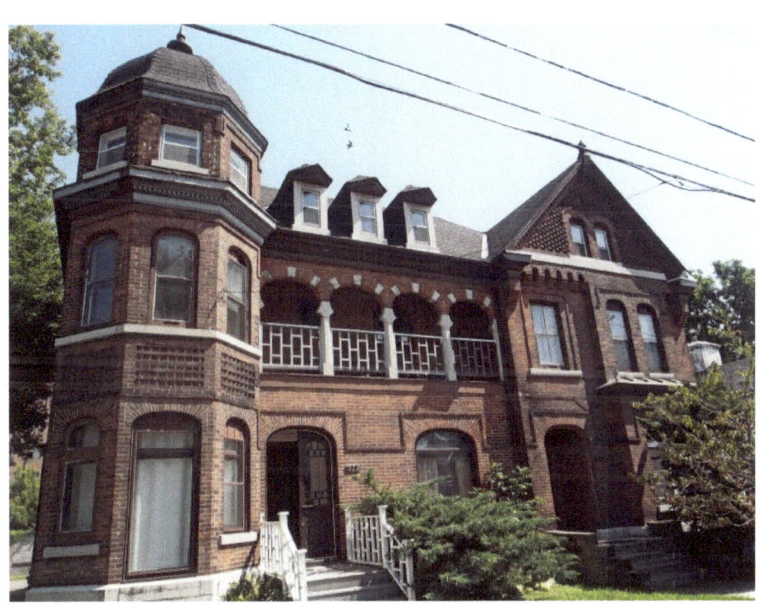

197-199 King Street East – Queen Anne – three-storey turret, dormers, second floor sleeping balcony, dichromatic voussoirs, decorative brickwork in large gable

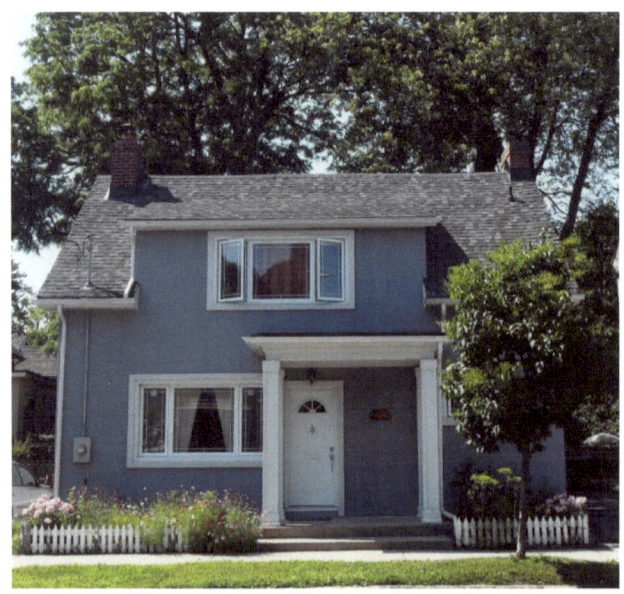

196 King Street East – shed dormer

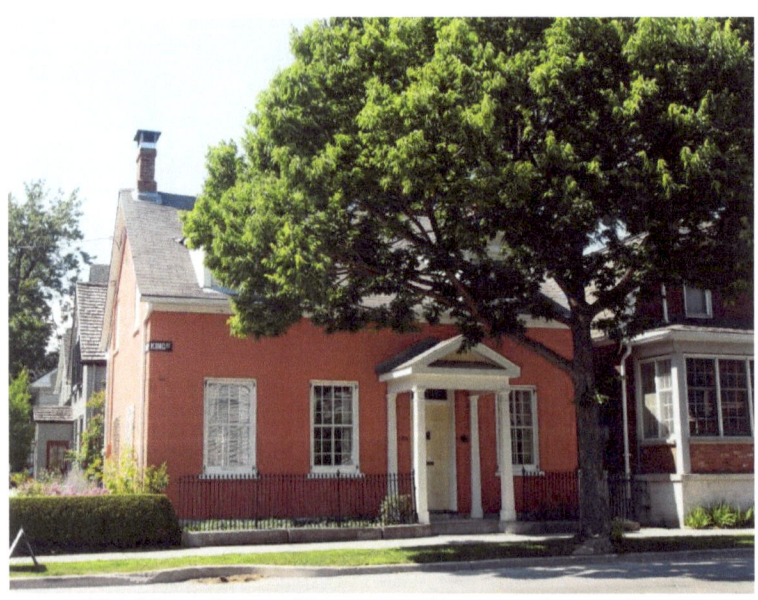

194 King Street East – pediment above door

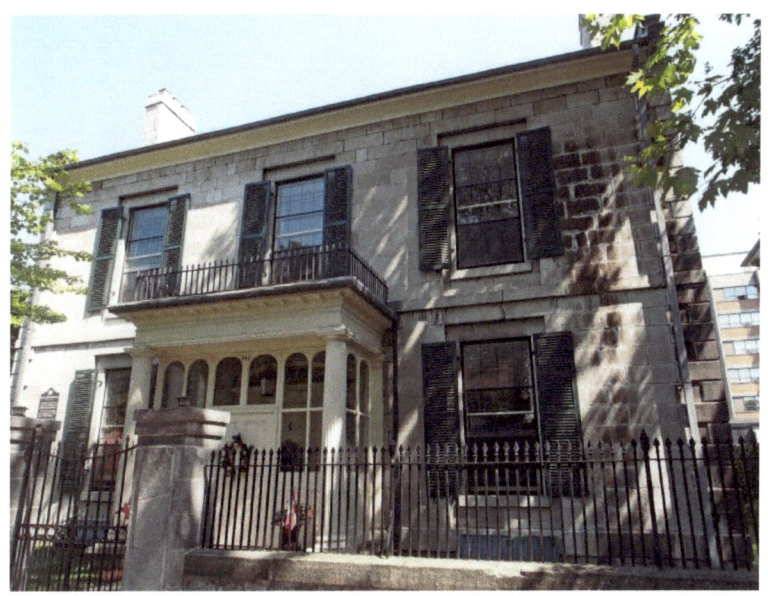

191 King Street East – Cartwright House – 1832-33
- Neoclassical - dressed stone blocks house - built for
Reverend Robert David Cartwright and his bride, Harriet
Dobbs of Dublin, Ireland

The appearance of the house has not changed since it was
built; even the fence in front is original.

Sir Richard Cartwright (December 24, 1835-1912) was born in
this house. He became Canadian Minister of Finance and
Minister of Trade and Commerce; he was an advocate of
unrestricted reciprocity with the United States; his father was
the Reverend David Cartwright, Chaplain to the forces and
curate of St. George's

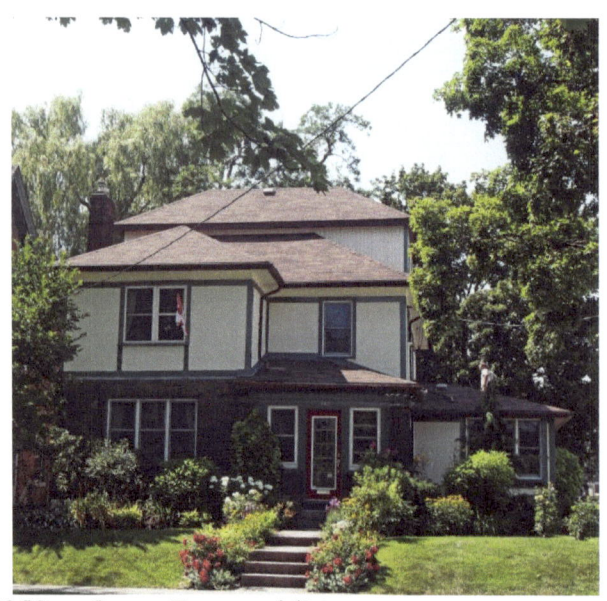

180 King Street East – additions to one storey cottage

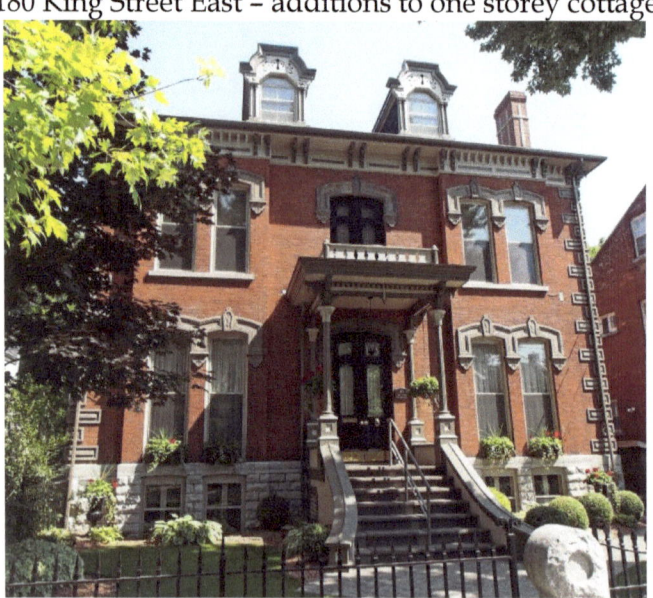

169 King Street East – designed in 1885 by William Newlands for banker Donald Fraser – three-bay, two-storey house is built on a high foundation; porch with paired columns on brick piers and a plain balustrade was added later; corner quoins with raised panels; channeled hood-moulds over all windows have decorative keystones and ends

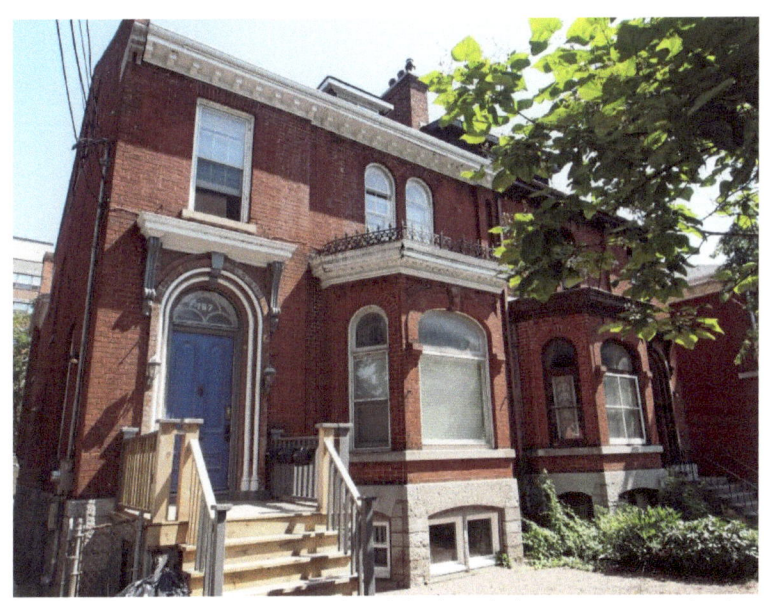

167-165 King Street East – double brick house commissioned by Richard Cartwright, designed by William Coverdale in 1858 as a rental property; paired windows with round heads in the second storey; fanlights; iron cresting above bay window

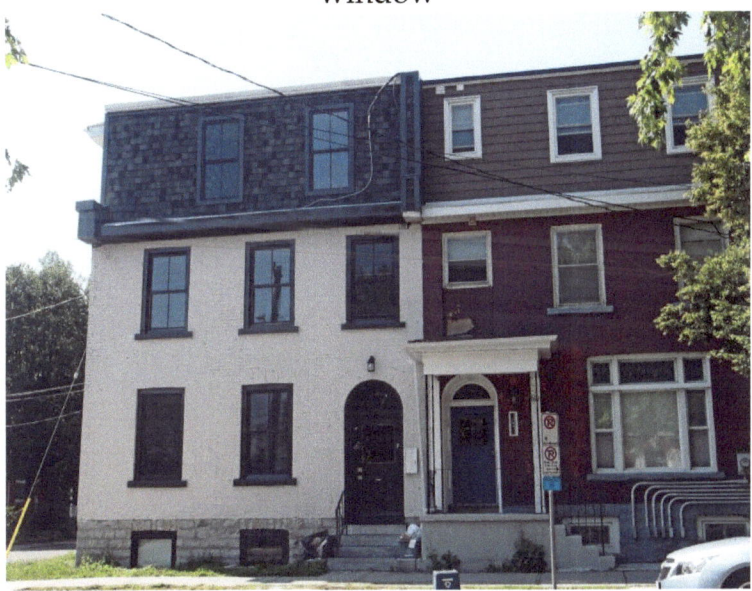

162 King Street East – transom windows above doors

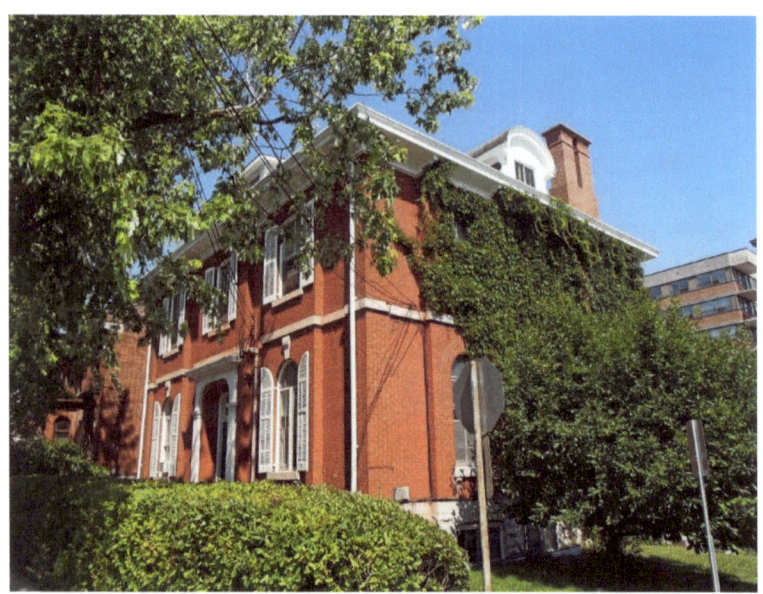

161 King Street East – two storey brick, dormers

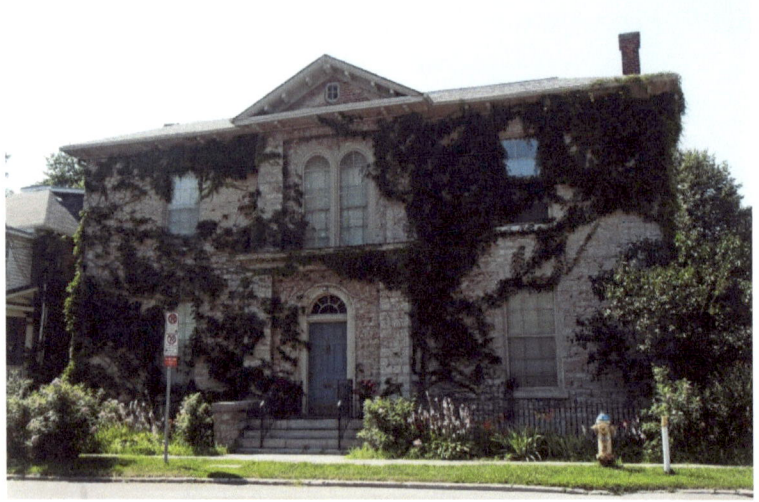

156 King Street East – Earl Place – 1851 – Italianate
- frontispiece topped with pediment with unique shaped
window, transom window above door

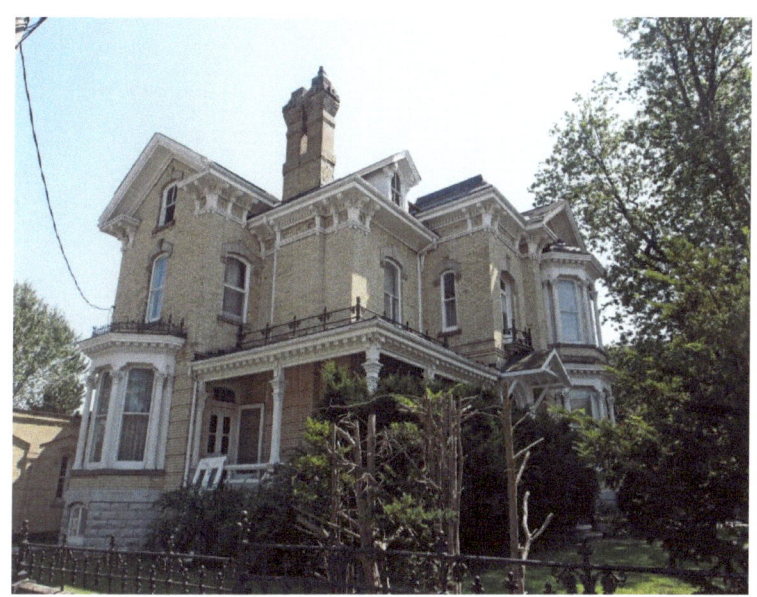

157 King Street East – 1882 – Victorian mansion – cornice brackets, two-storey bay topped with gable with cornice return feature, dormer, iron cresting on second floor, dentil moulding, bay windows have columns around the windows with Corinthian capitals

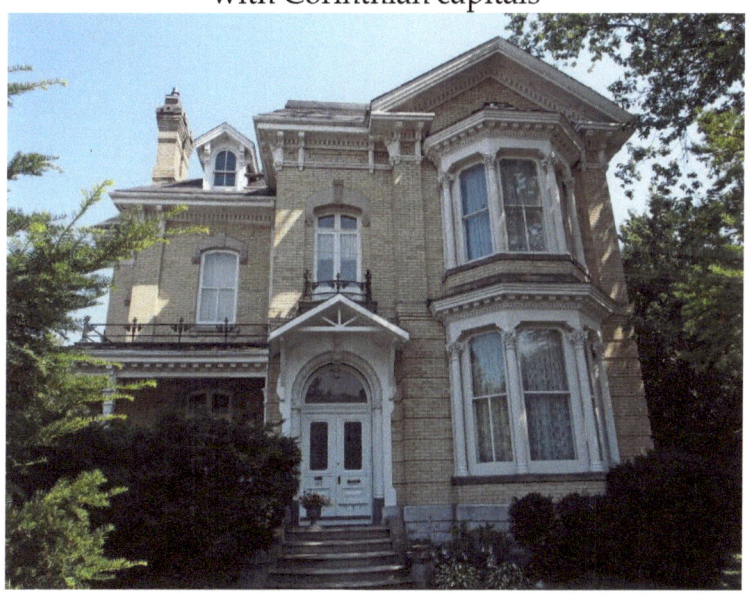

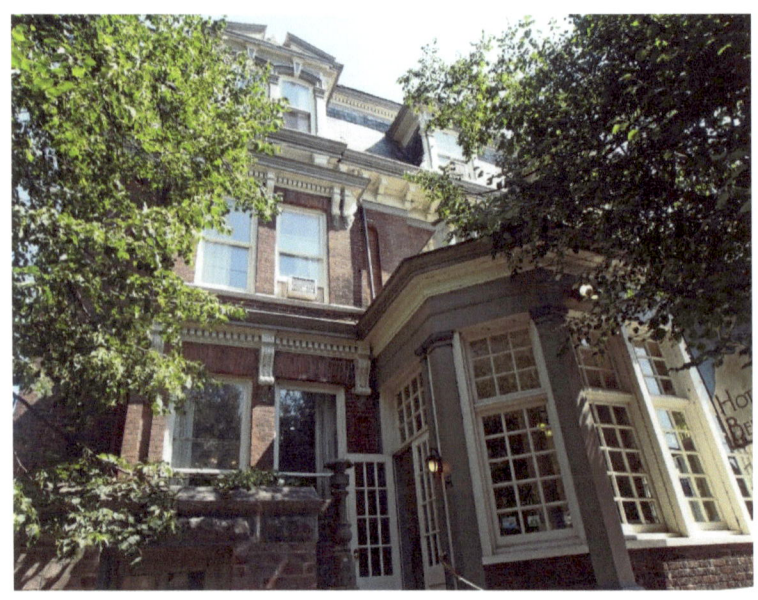

141 King Street East – 1880 – Hotel Belvedere - Second Empire style, slate mansard roof, dormers, bay window, dentil moulding, cornice brackets; brick and stone are used

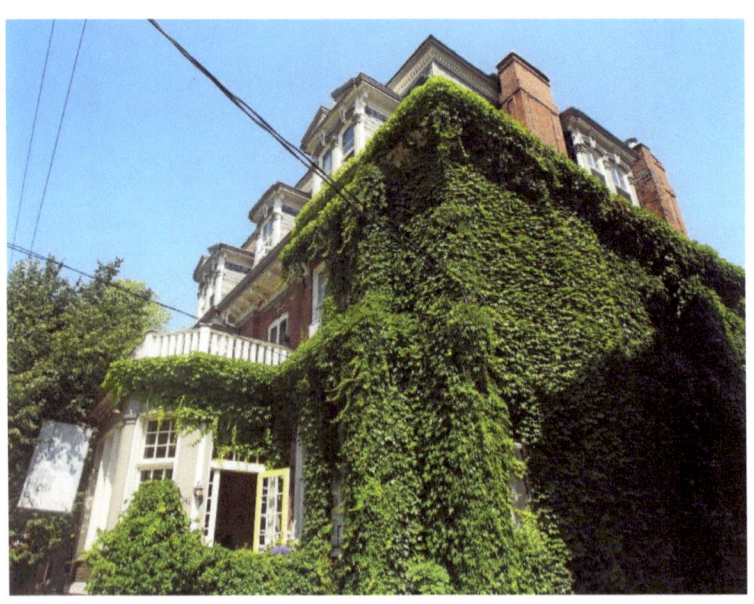

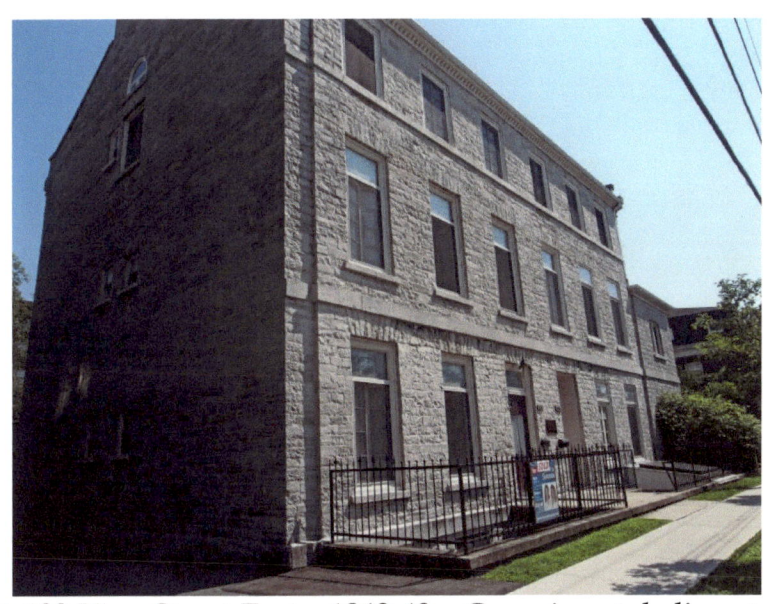

131-133 King Street East – 1842-43 – Georgian style limestone
double house, notable for its windows and
ashlar string courses

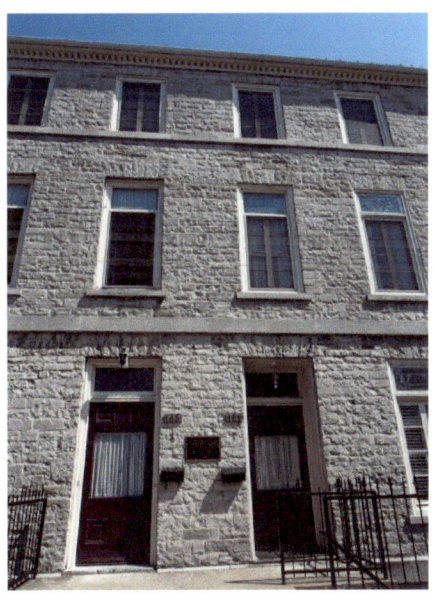

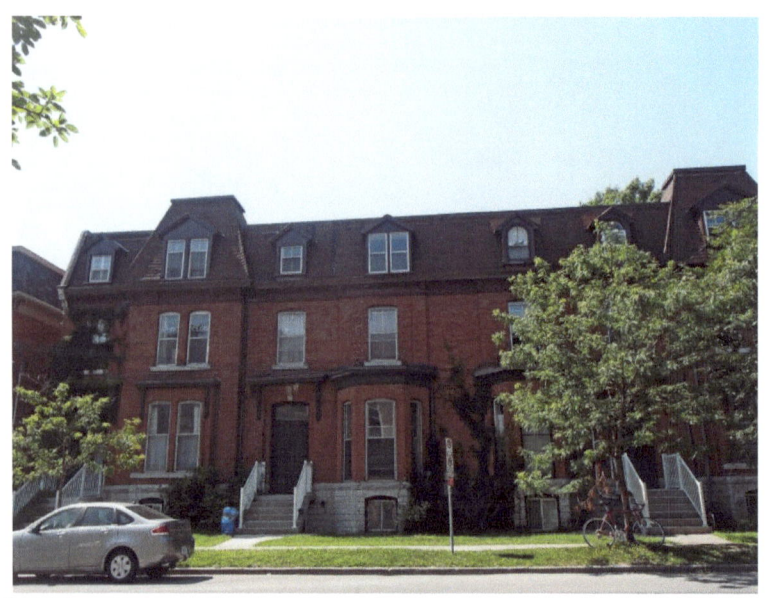

134 King Street East – Second Empire style – mansard roof with dormers, bay windows

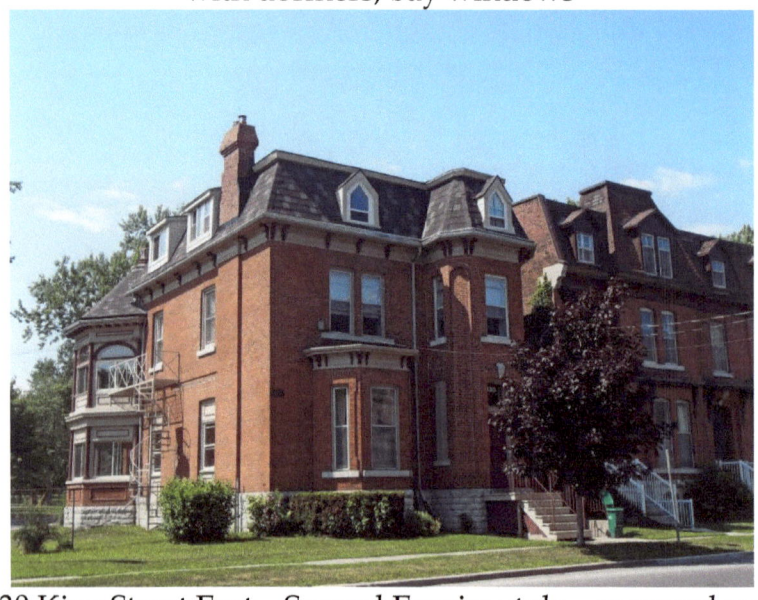

130 King Street East – Second Empire style – mansard roof with dormers, two-storey tower-like bay windows, cornice brackets

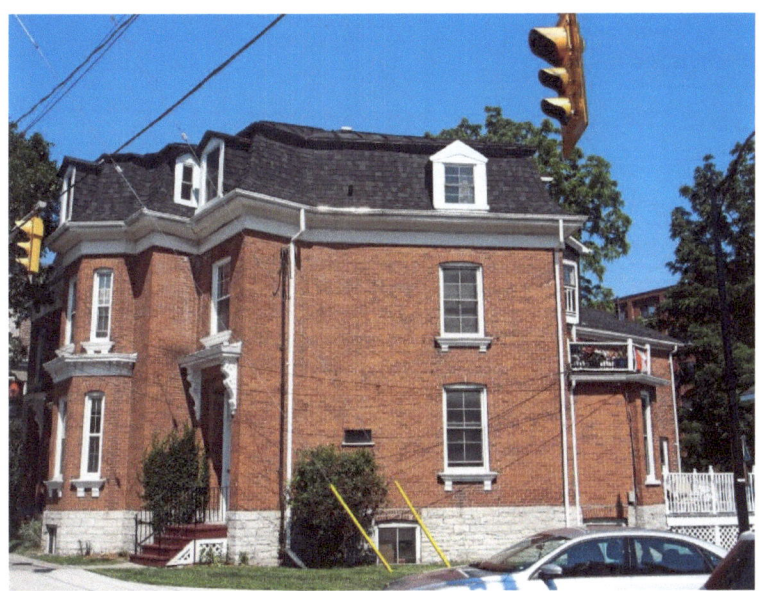

125 King Street East – Second Empire style, mansard roof with dormers

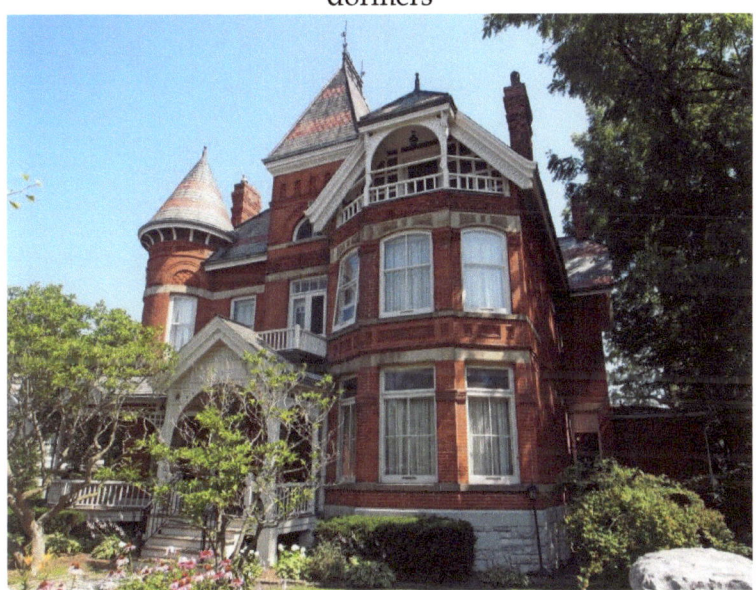

95 King Street East – Hendry House – 1886 – high Victorian house in Queen Anne style – asymmetrical design, variety of roof heights and construction materials; terra cotta (hard kiln-fired clay) panels; third floor sleeping porch, turret; dichromatic tile work

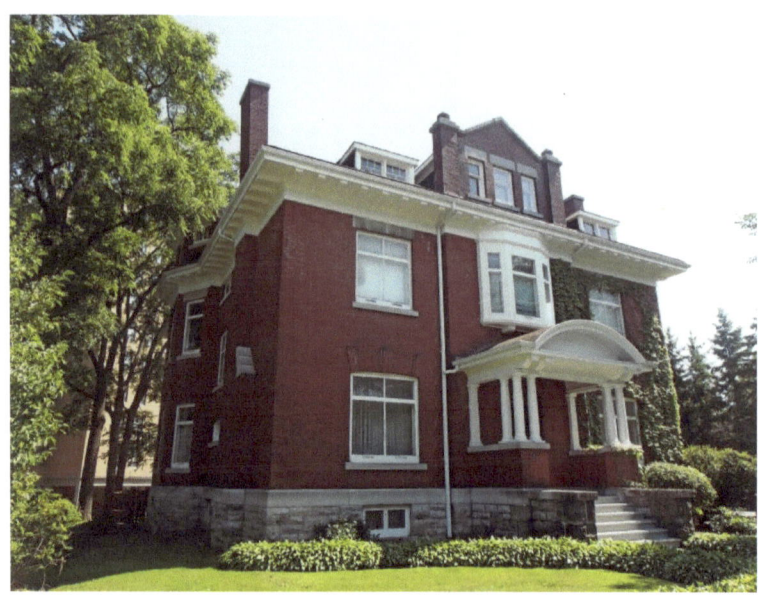

87 King Street East – Italianate – columns with Doric capitals, dormers, centre one with pediment

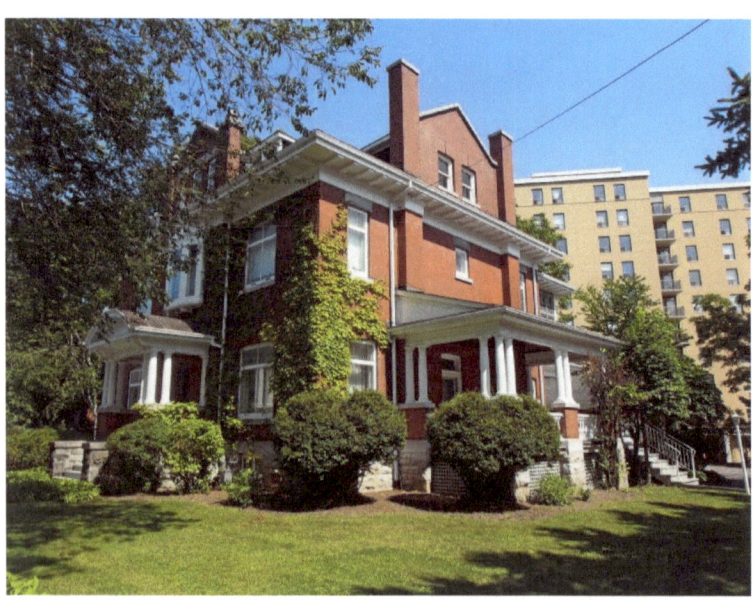

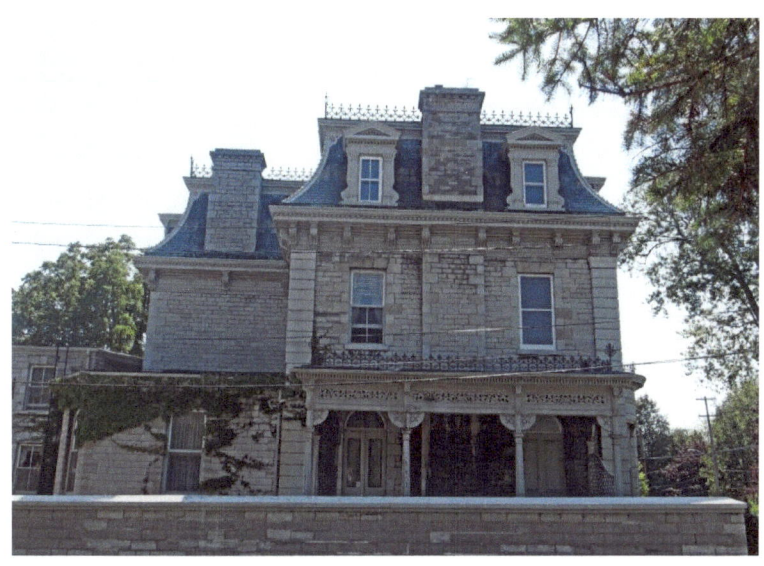

85 King Street East – 1877 – three storey Victorian Second Empire style stone mansion – mansard roof, dormers, verandah, bay windows

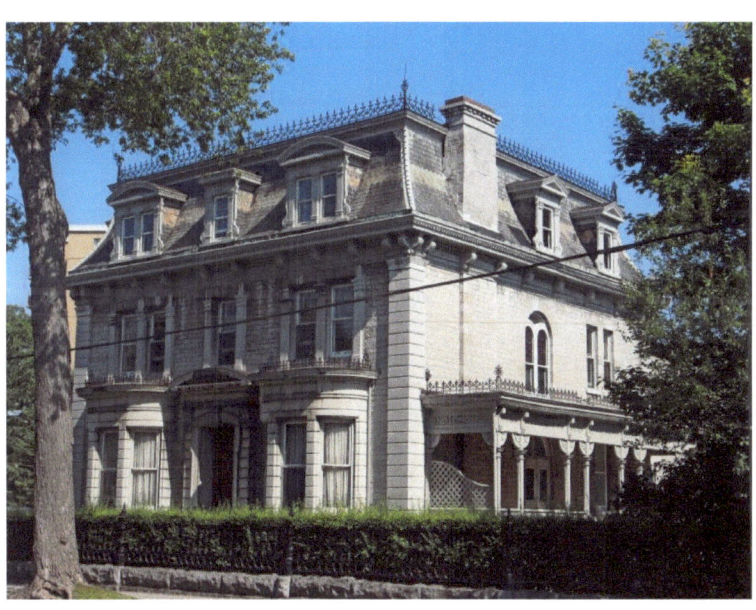

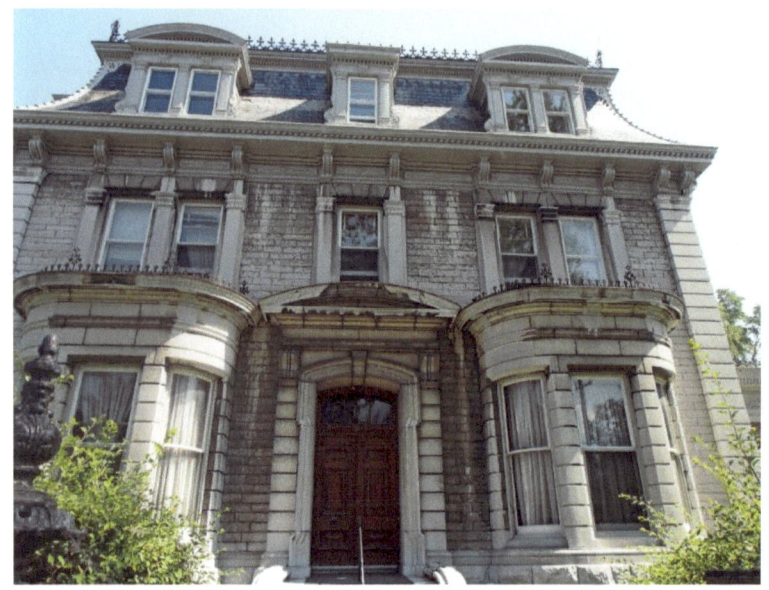

85 King Street East – iron cresting above bay windows, and on rooftop, cornice brackets, transom window above door

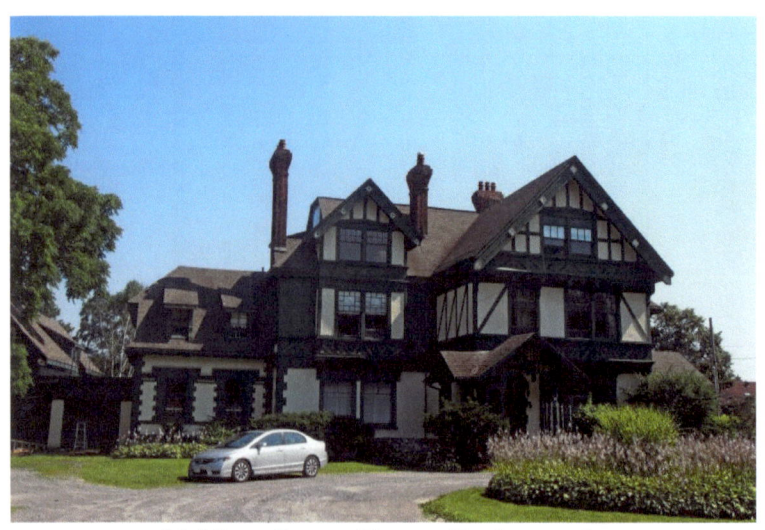

81 King Street East – Tudor style

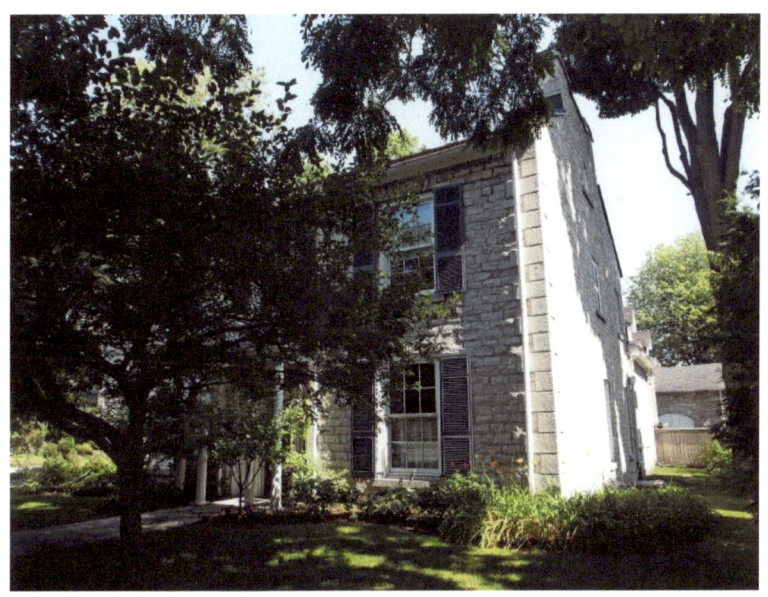

53 King Street East

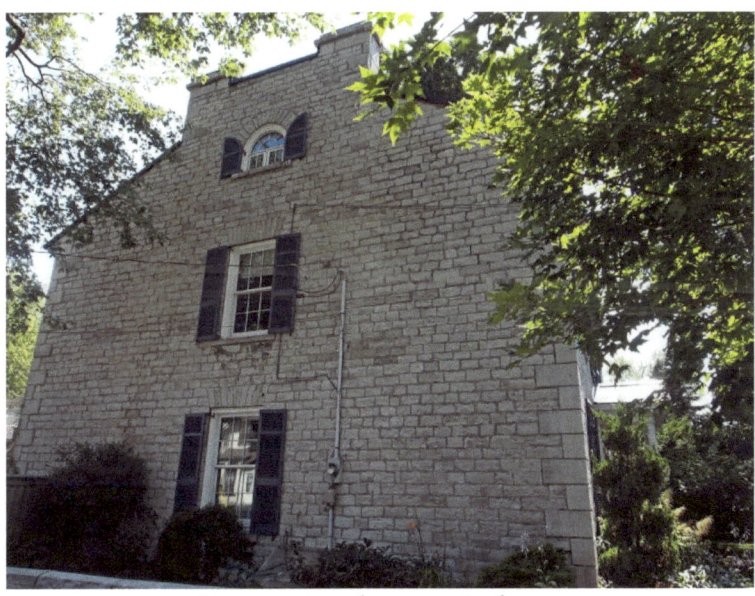

Voussoirs above windows

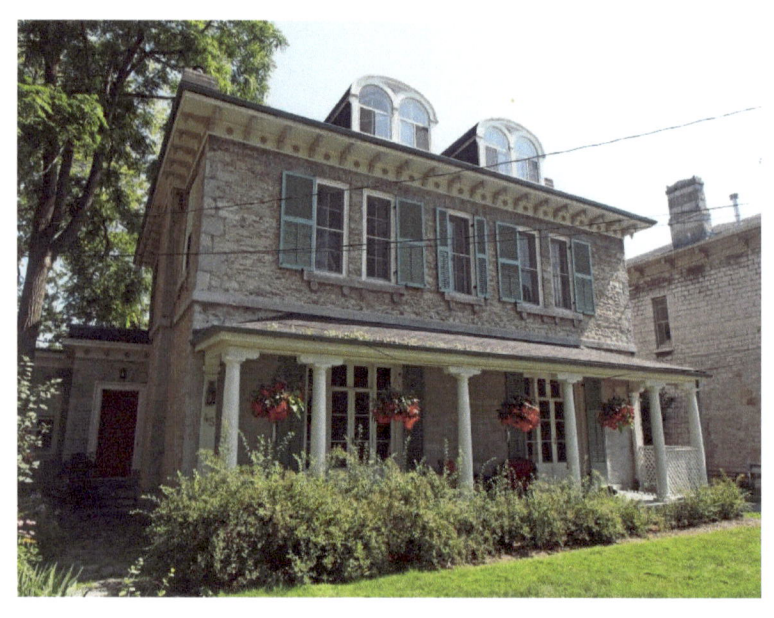

45 King Street East

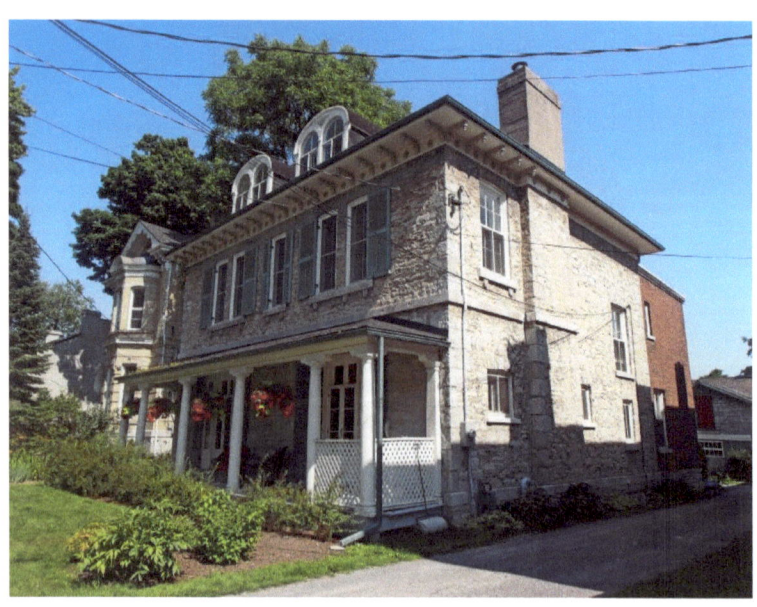

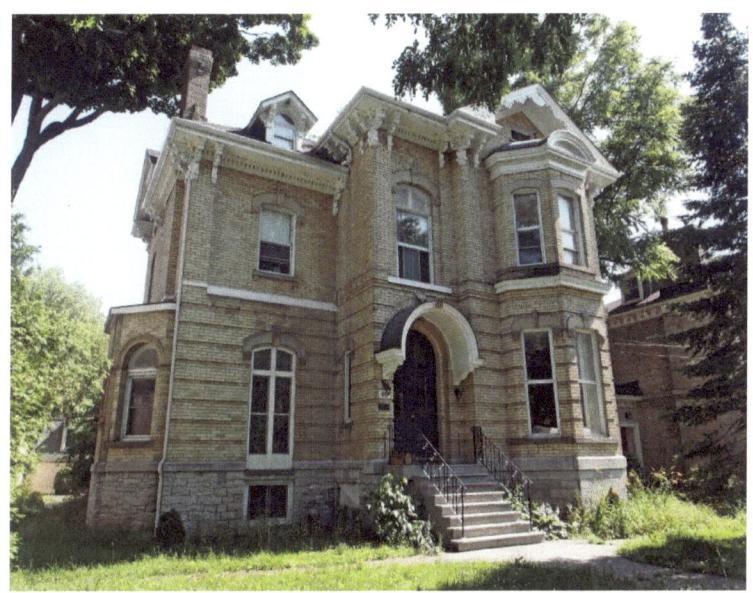

49 King Street East – Victorian mansion – slightly smaller and less elaborate than #157 – cornice brackets, dormers, two-storey tower-like bay

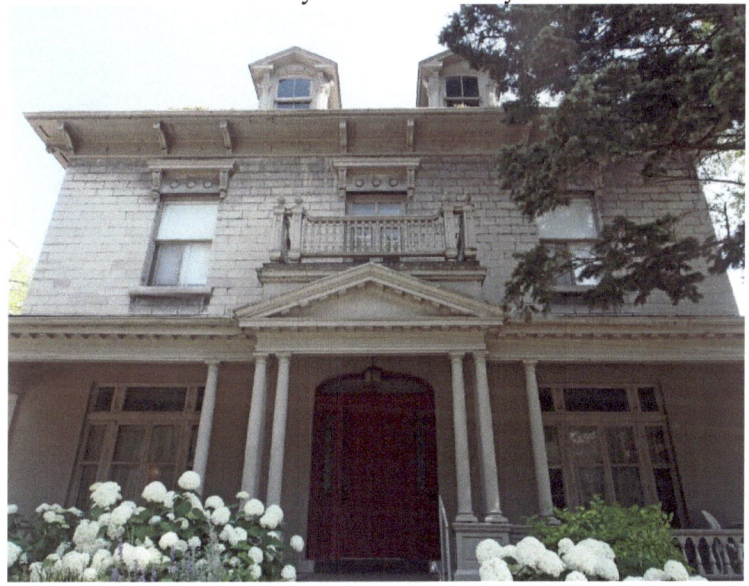

31 King Street East – Parkview House – 1853 – two-storey stone dwelling in the Cottage Orné style popular in the 1850s

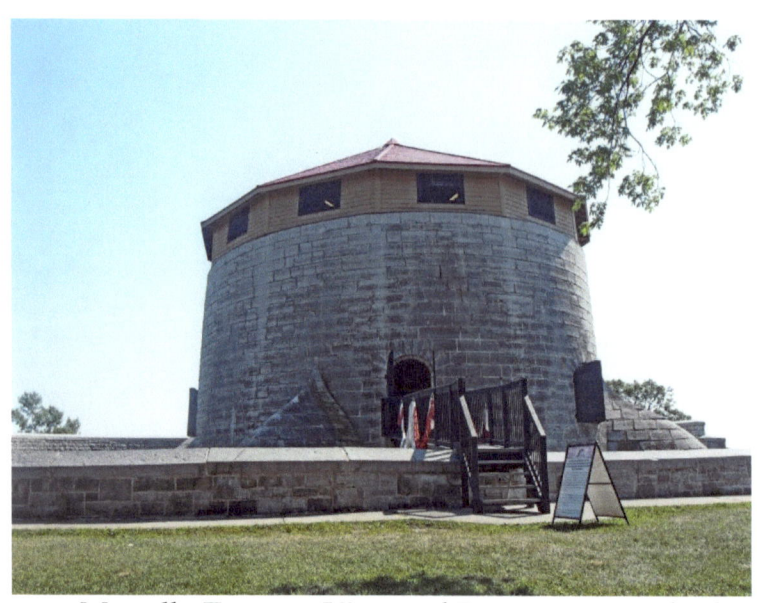

Murney Martello Tower – King and Barrie Streets – built 1846 at the height of the Oregon crisis - the 1846 Oregon Treaty established the border between British North America and the United States along the 49th parallel

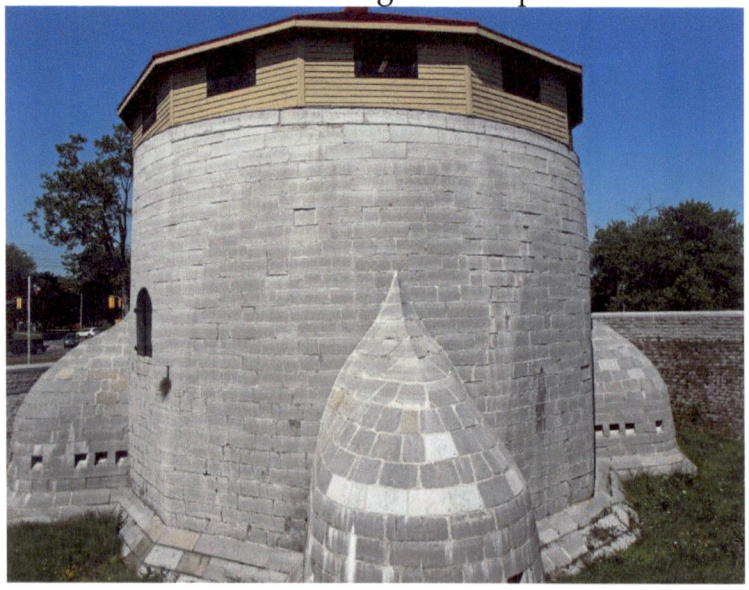

Oneida was equipped and sent upon the lake in the fall of 1810, operating from Sackets Harbor, New York, near the beginning of the St. Lawrence, while the British port of Kingston lay nearly opposite in Canada. On November 10, 1812 a naval engagement was fought at the entrance to Kingston harbour between H.M.S. Royal George and U.S.S. Oneida supported by American schooners. *Royal George* cut her mooring cables and finally made fast to a wharf under the protection of troop muskets. *Royal George* suffered extensive damage, and *Oneida* had some damage with one seaman killed and three wounded, but a gale ended the engagement.

Murney Martello Tower

This tower was built on Murney Point in 1846 as the westernmost part of the Kingston fortification system – part of the new naval defences – during the Oregon Crisis of 1845-46. Its guns were intended to cover the approaches from Lake Ontario. It was one of the last British works of defence begun in the Canadian interior and is one of the most sophisticated of the Martello towers built in British North America.

Three other Martello towers and Fort Henry survive today and represent the significance of Kingston to the defence of British North America.

Although in regular use as a barracks after 1849, it was not fully armed until 1862 when it had already become obsolete because of rapid advance in offensive military technology.

The tower was abandoned by the military in 1885. In 1925 the Kingston Historical Society re-opened the tower as a museum. There are three floors of exhibits that depict the life of the soldier and his family in the nineteenth century.

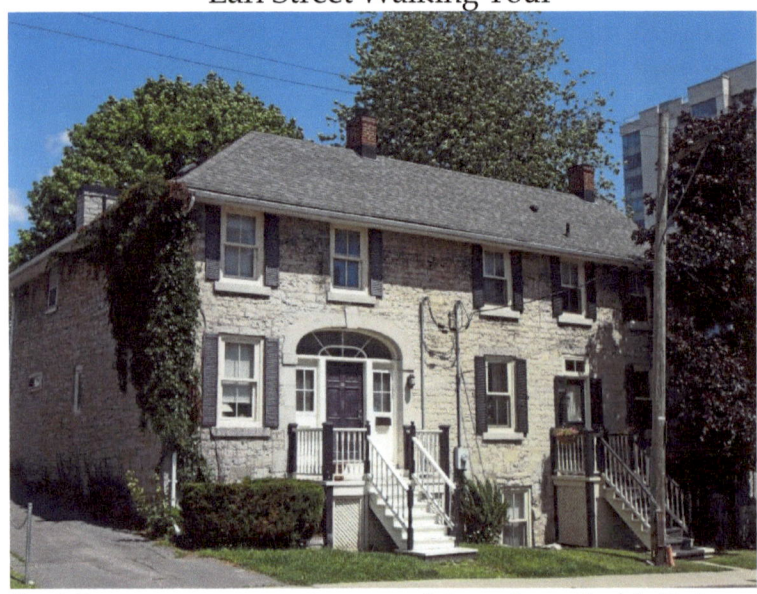

28 Earl Street – two storey stone, hipped roof, sidelights and transom window

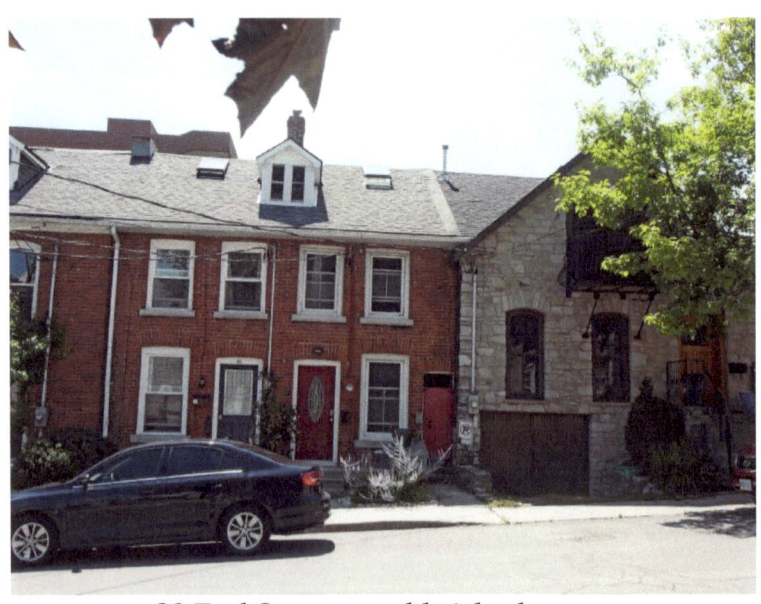

20 Earl Street – red brick, dormer

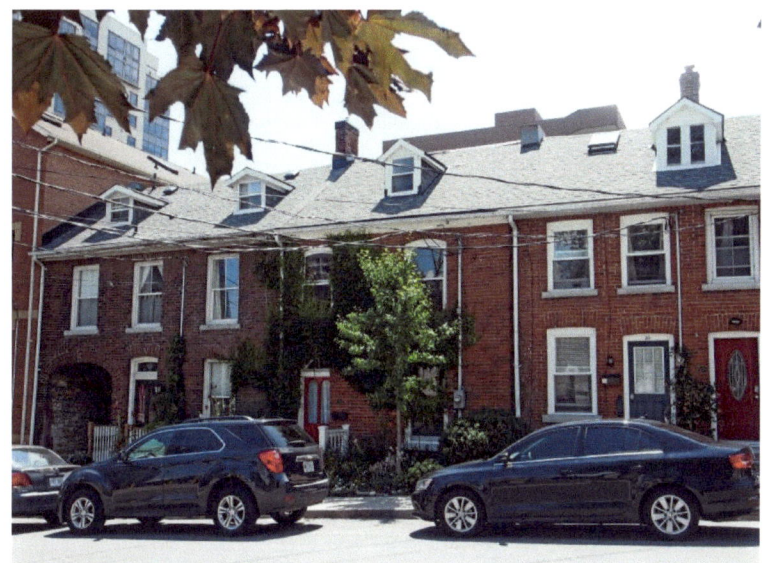

16-20 Earl Street – row of brick homes for employees of the Locomotive Works, flour mill, shipyard and other industries that used to be on Ontario Street

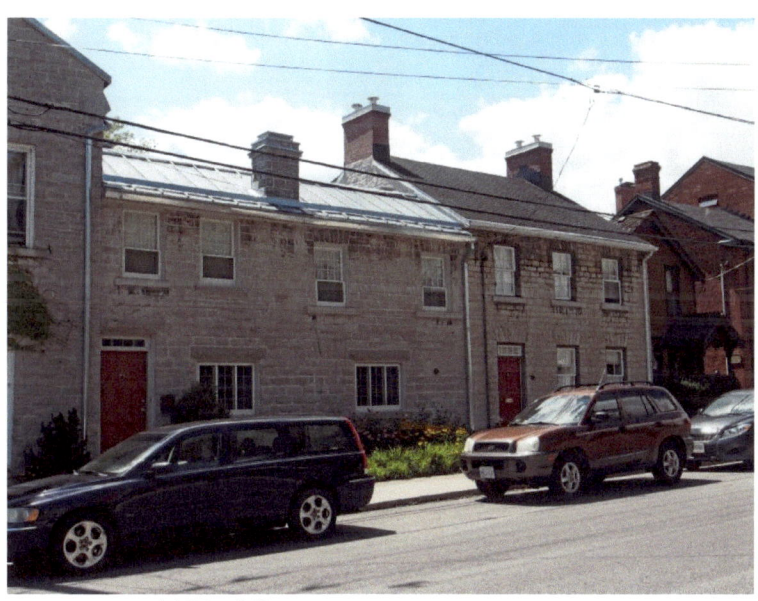

44 Earl Street – two storeys, stone

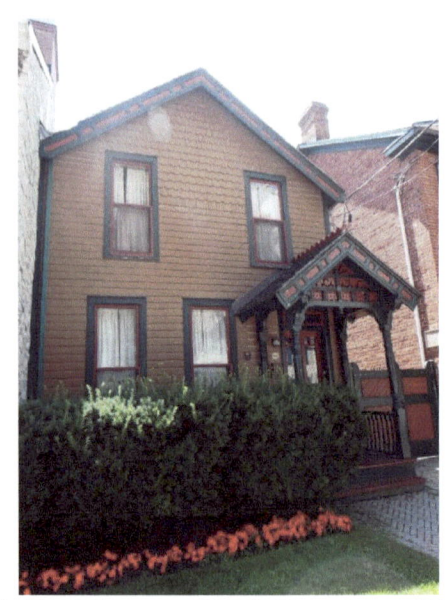

48 Earl Street – Reid Cottage – 1880

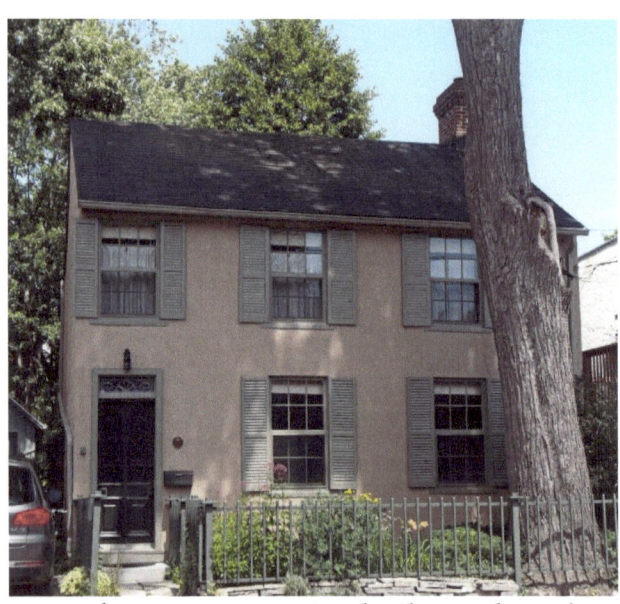

47 Earl Street – frame construction built as a boarding house in 1841 – the wood is now covered by stucco

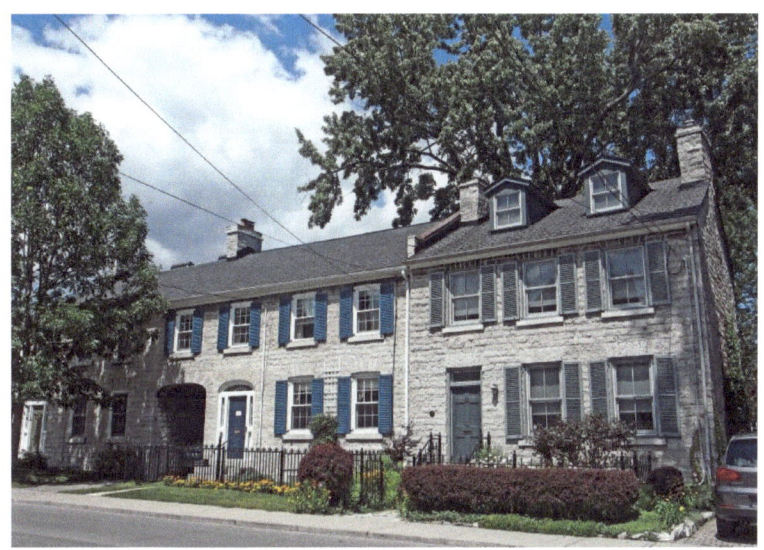

49-55 Earl Street – #49 was a single house built about 1834; #53-55 were built about 1844 – designed by Thomas Rogers, the first architect to settle in Kingston; #53 was the home of the owner, an engineer, and he built #55 to rent out

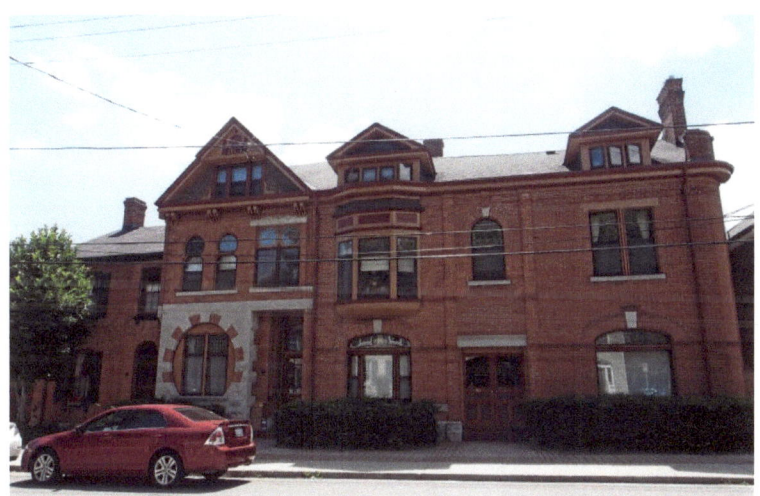

50-56 Earl Street - #56 (on the right – west – side) was built in 1905 – the doorway and windows all have different shapes

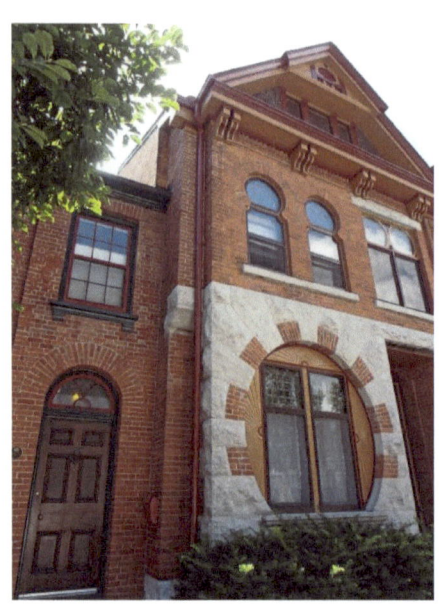

52 Earl Street – built by William Henry Smith in 1876
– Grove House – sunburst design on the façade; cornice
brackets, oriel window, dormers

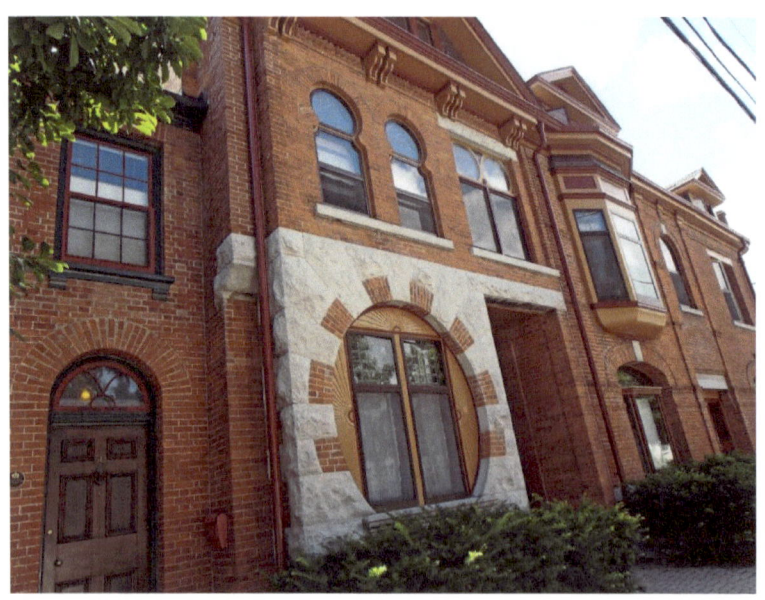

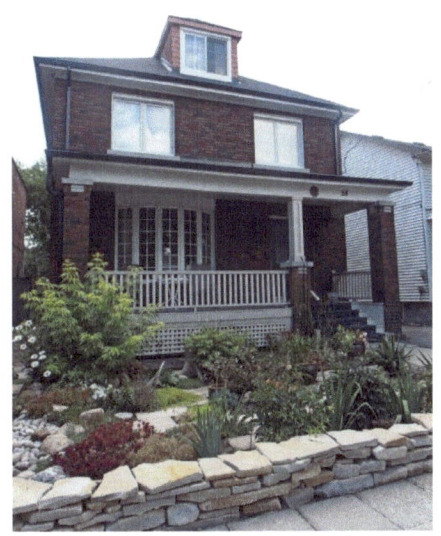

58 Earl Street – hipped roof, dormer

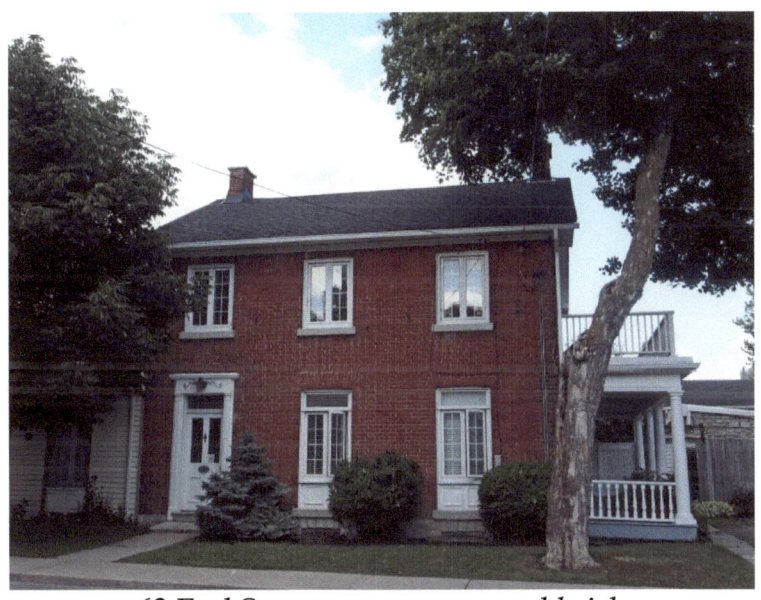

63 Earl Street – two storey red brick

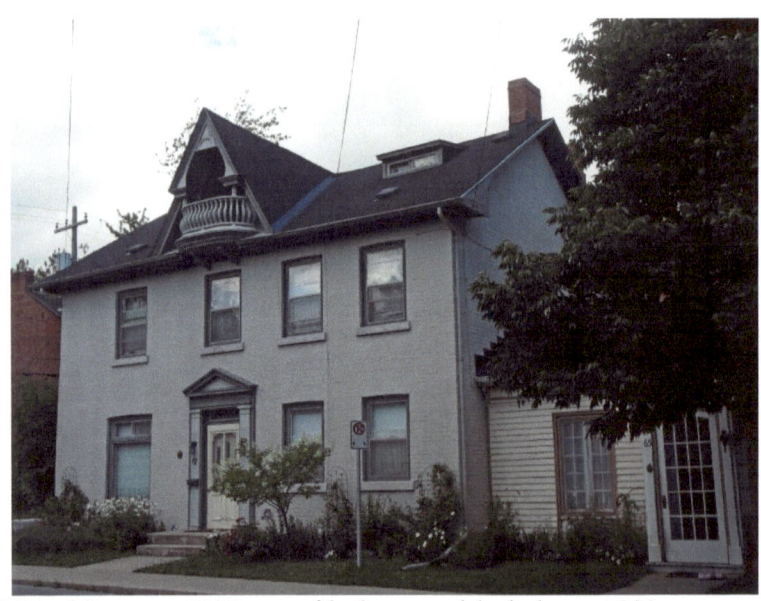

67 Earl Street – 1847 – roof balcony added about 1900, two roof dormers added about 1960 – Joseph Hanley and his descendants lived in this house from 1858 to about 1950 – Grand Trunk Railway and steamship ticket agents; pediment, transom window

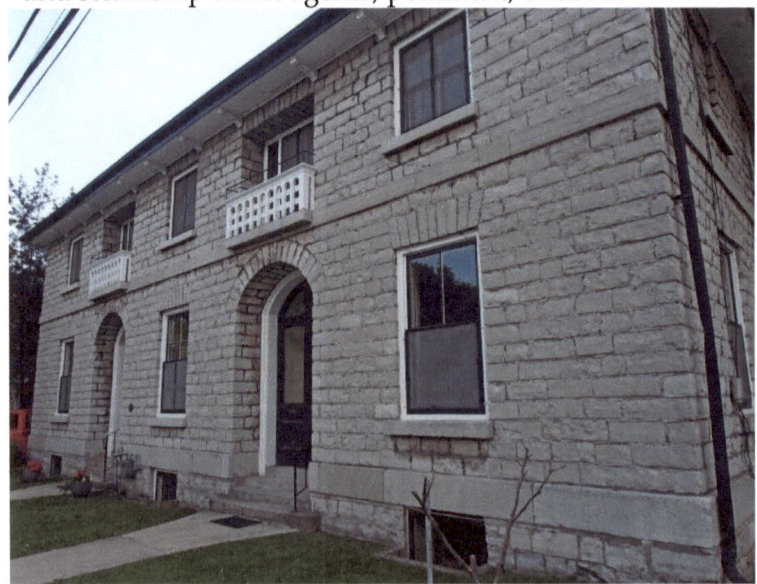

66-68 Earl Street – built 1842 – doors with curved tops with "Venetian" windows above them

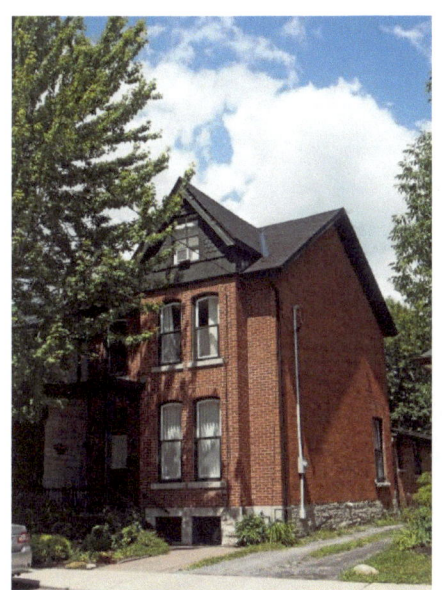

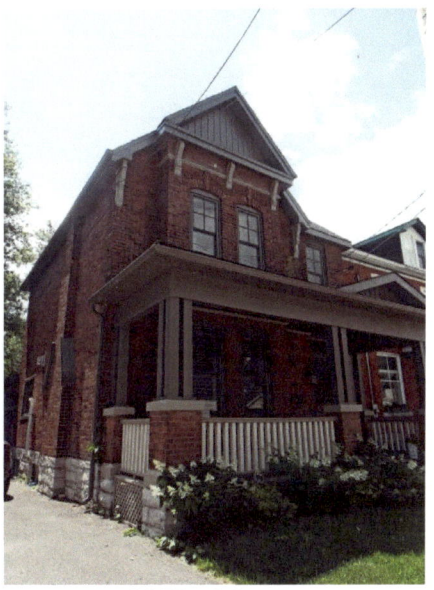

81 Earl Street
2 storey Gothic, dormer

80 Earl Street
cornice brackets

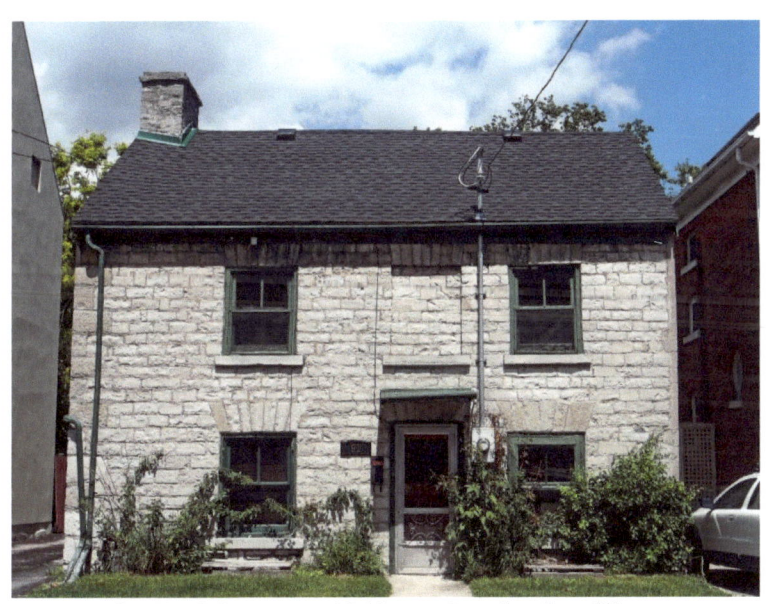

91 Earl Street – 1840s – simple dwelling

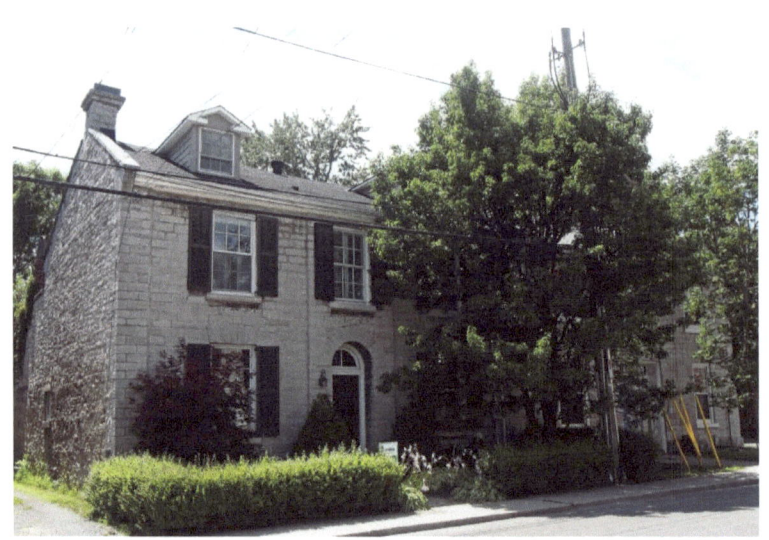

98 Earl Street – Gothic – stone, dormer

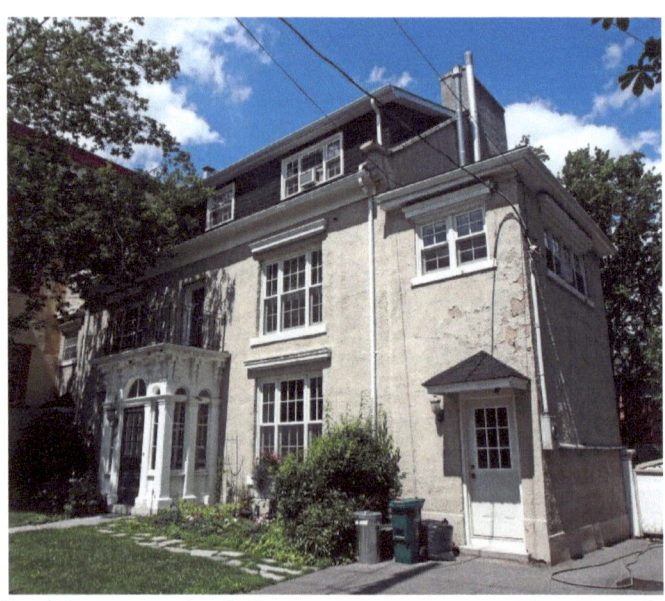

117 Earl Street – shed dormer, entrance with second-floor balcony above

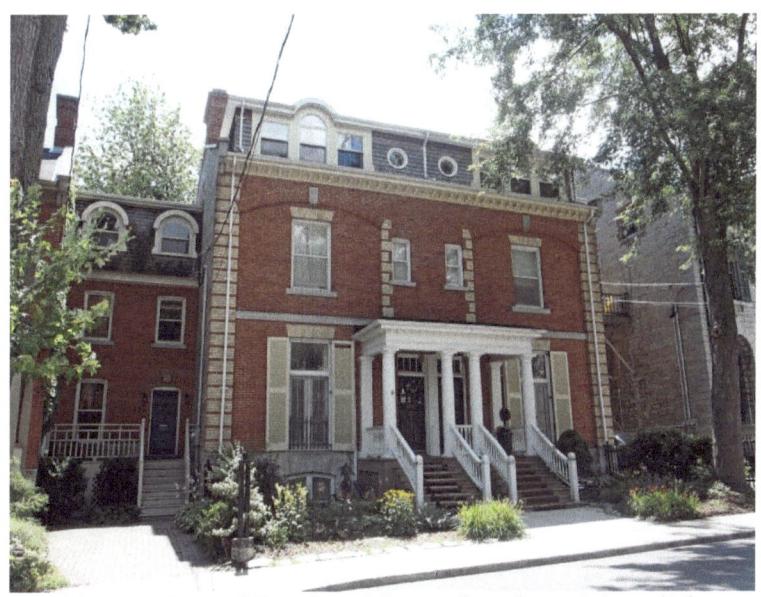

126 Earl Street – Second Empire – Mansard roof, quoining, dichromatic brickwork, window hoods, voussoirs with keystones, transom windows, columns with Doric capitals

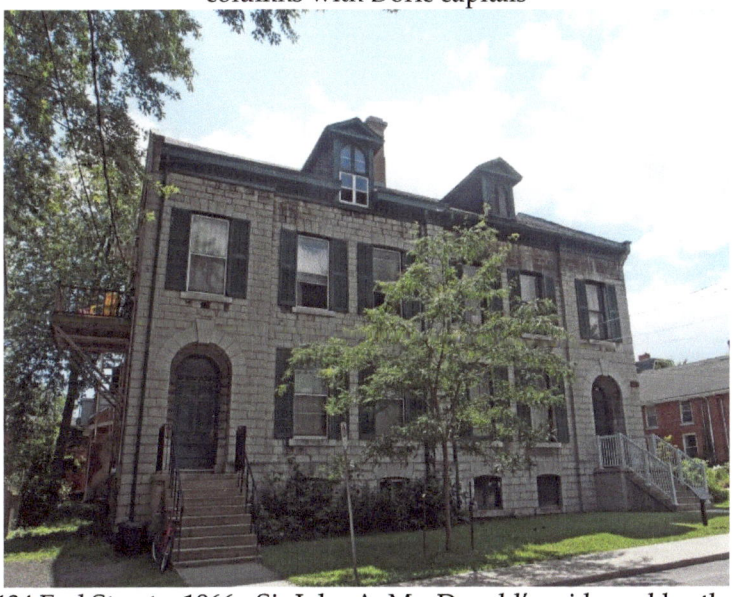

132-134 Earl Street – 1866 - Sir John A. MacDonald's widowed brother-in-law, James Williamson, a professor at Queen's, and Sir John's unmarried sister Louisa resided at #134;
dormers, voussoirs with keystones over doors

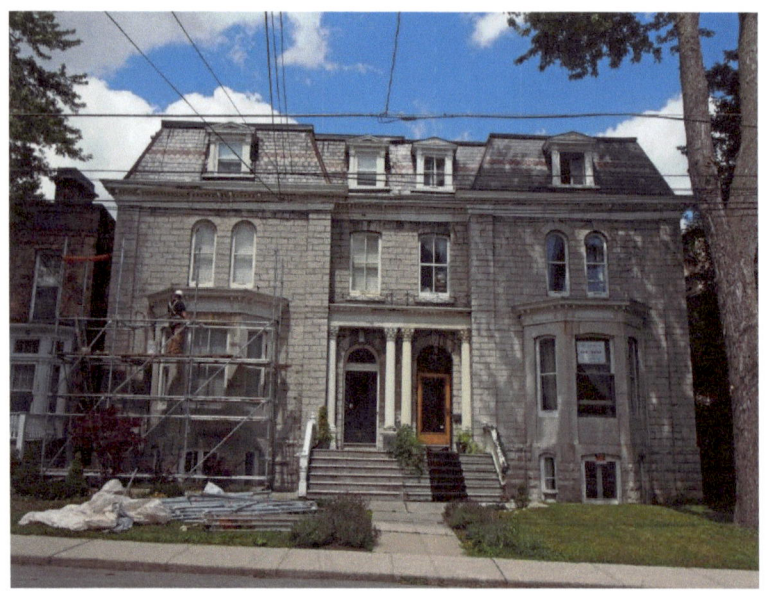

149-151 Earl Street - 1873-74 – Second Empire style - mansard roof with dormers, high basement, three storeys; dichromatic slate shingles, dentil moulding, cornice brackets, Corinthian capitals on columns surrounding doors, bay windows

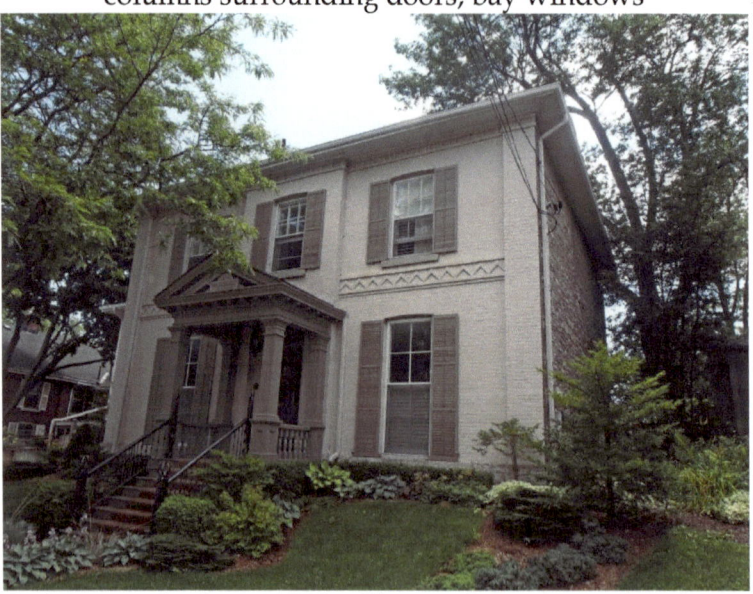

148 Earl Street – built in 1870 by Thomas Moore, a tailor; decorative brickwork; pediment with tympanum design; dentil moulding

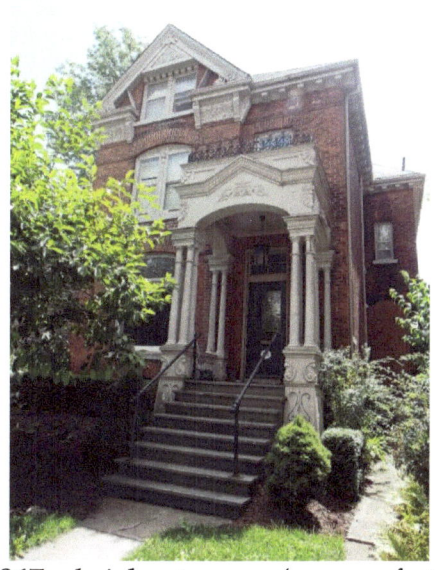

Earl Street – 1867 – brick – terrace (a row of attached houses that look alike) - tower

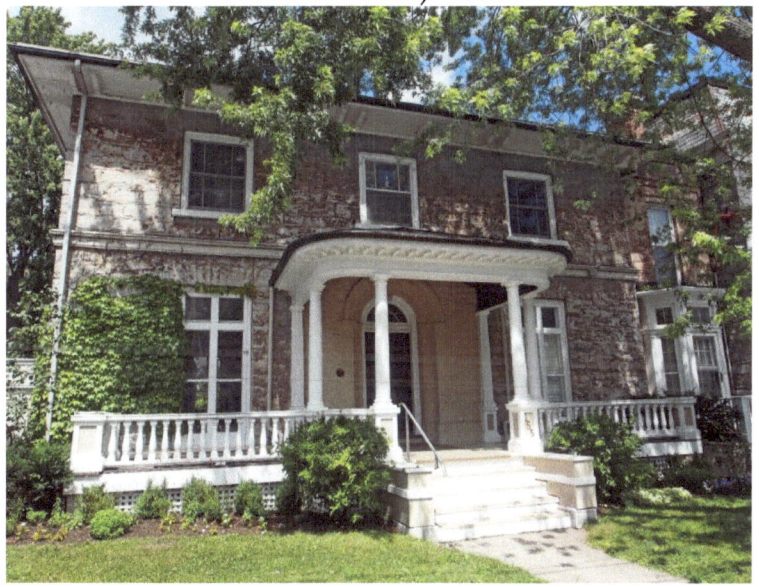

155 Earl Street – Kerr House – built 1848-49 – John Kerr, manager of the gas works, lived here from 1854-1904 – it was once painted red and then gray – traces of those colours remain

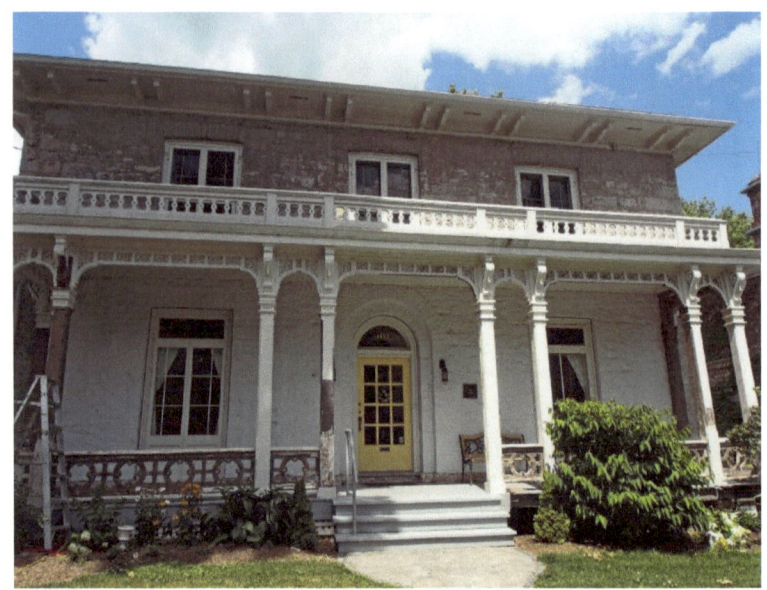

161 Earl Street – 1847 – built for John Fraser, Merchant in the wholesale hardware business; he and his wife Catherine Mowat had 10 children – second floor balcony

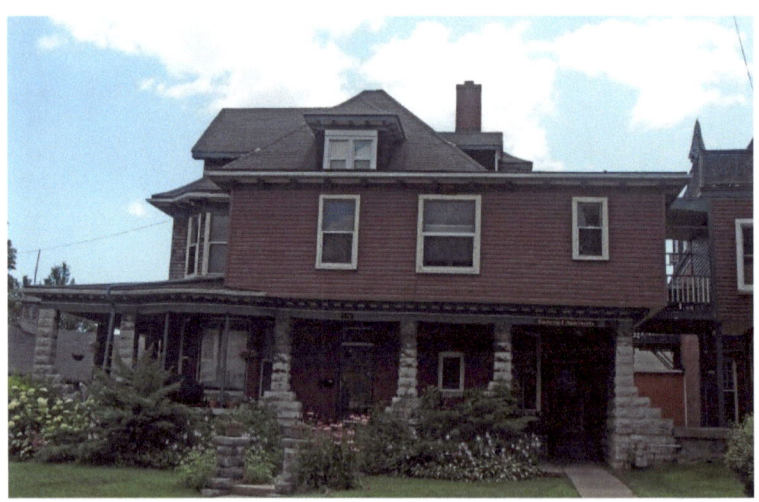

170 Earl Street – wraparound verandah, dormers

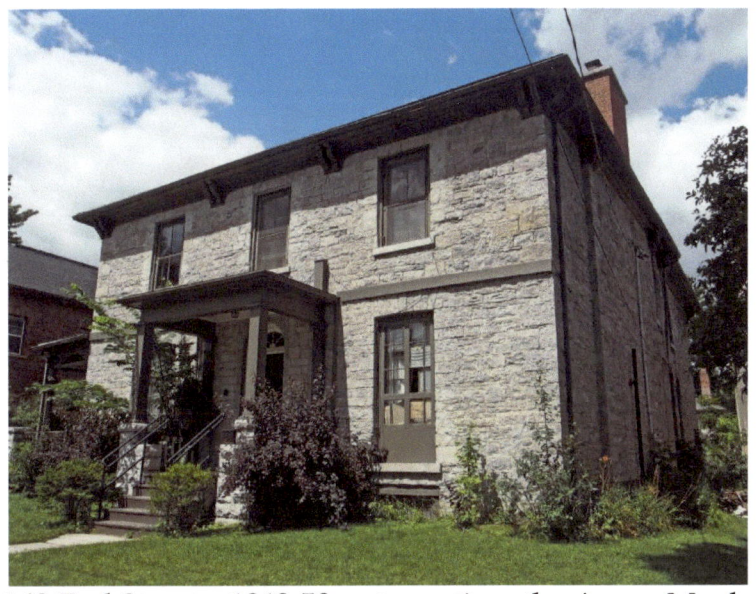

169 Earl Street – 1849-50 – at one time the Agnes Maule Machar Home for Protestant Women – two storey limestone, paired cornice brackets

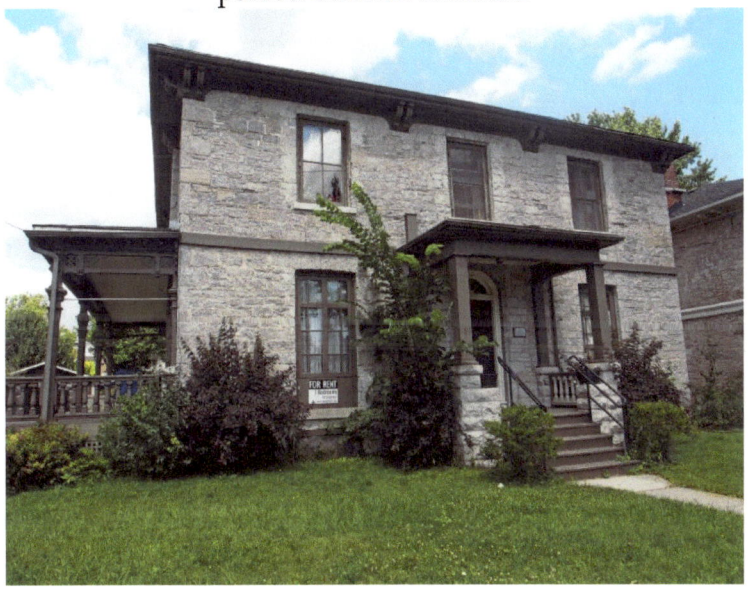

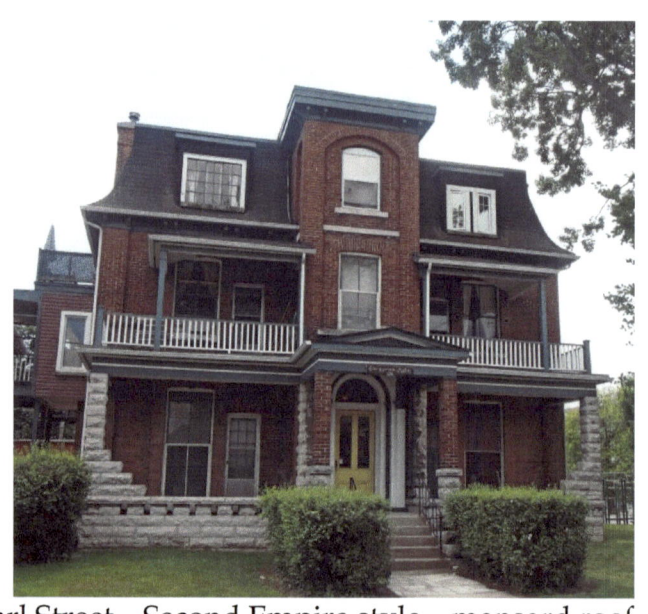

174 Earl Street – Second Empire style – mansard roof, three-storey frontispiece, second floor balconies, pediment, transom window

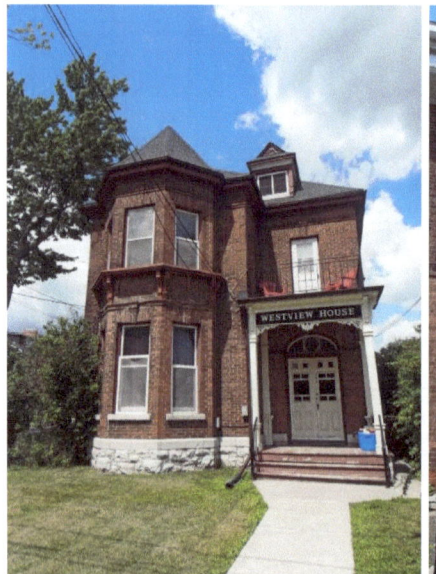
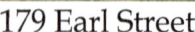

179 Earl Street

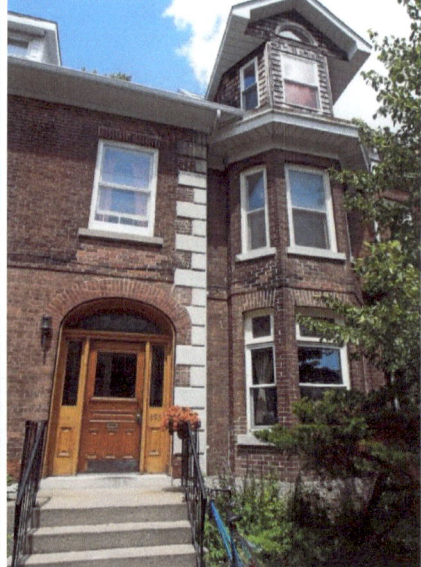

195 Earl Street – corner quoin, dormer above two-storey bay window

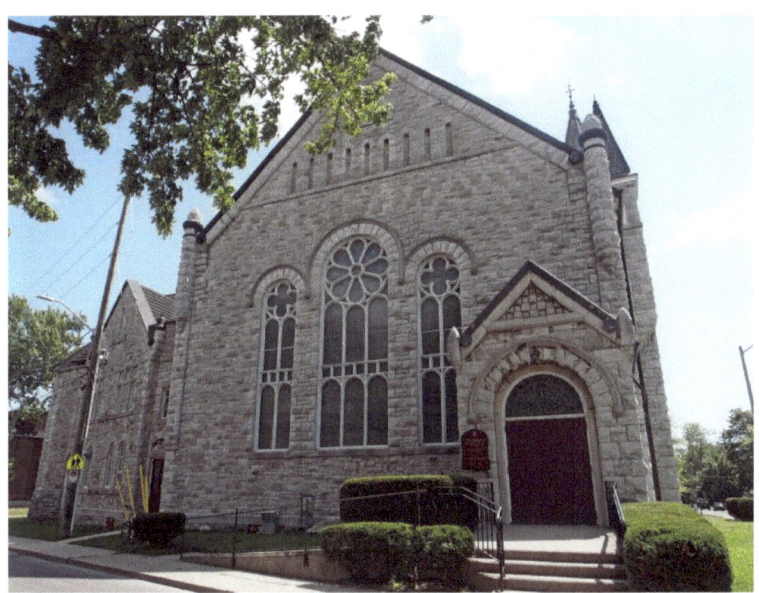

212 Barrie Street - In 1890, Chalmers Free Presbyterian Church was planned at the triangle of land formed by Barrie, Clergy and Earl Streets. The Union of the Congregational Church, Methodist Church and Presbyterian Church took place in 1925, electing to join Chalmers. Romanesque Revival style – rounded windows, rose window and quatrefoil windows, tower

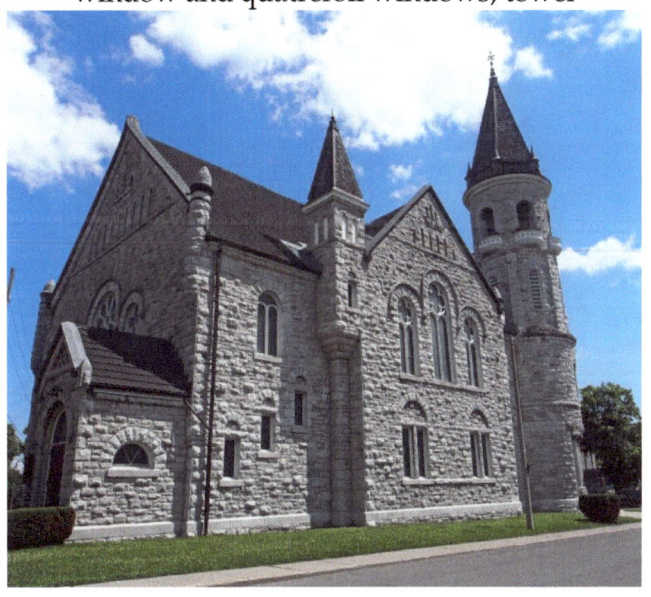

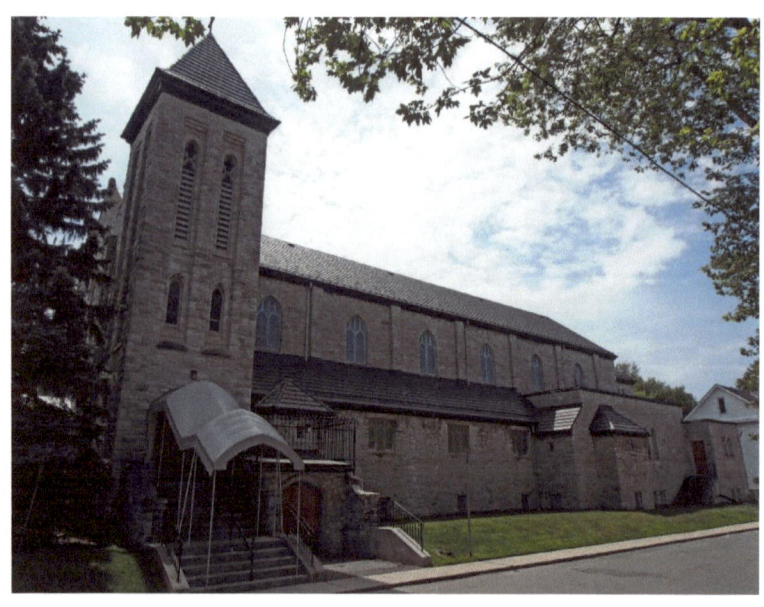

Patrick Street – St. John the Apostle Roman Catholic Church - limestone

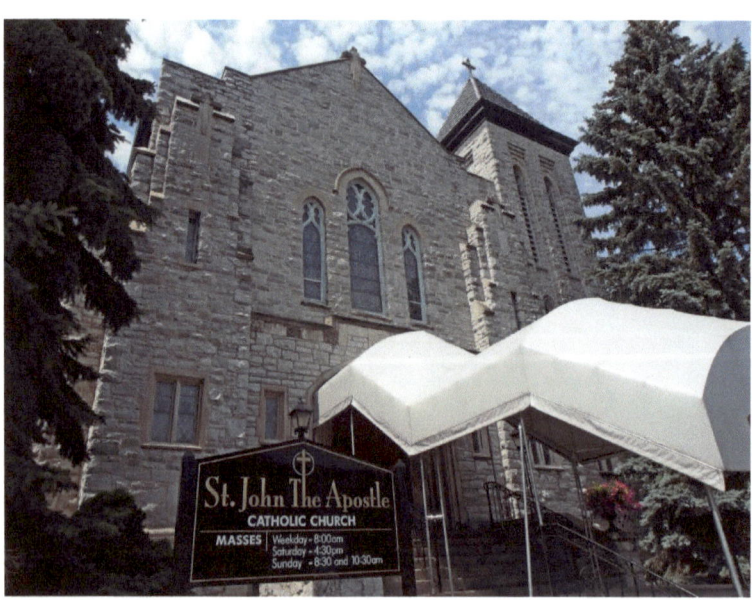

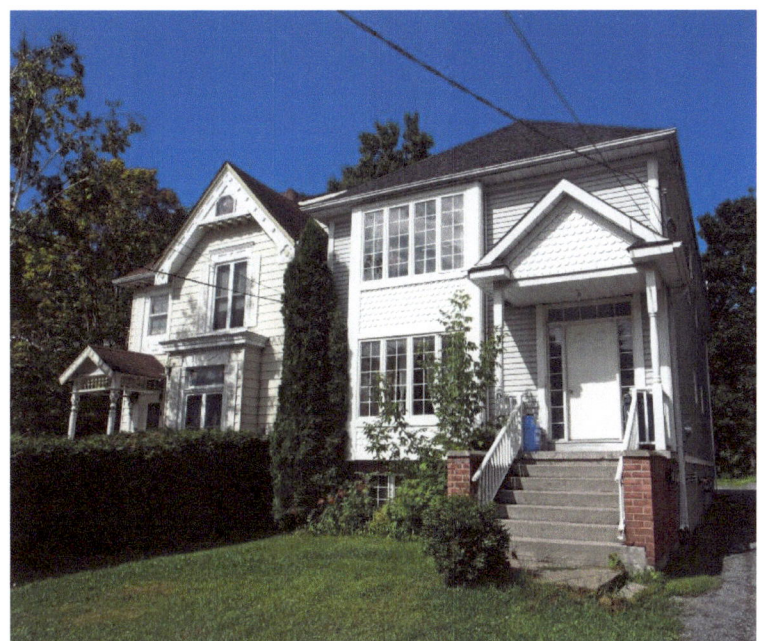

Pembroke Street – cornice return on pediment above door, sidelights and transom windows,

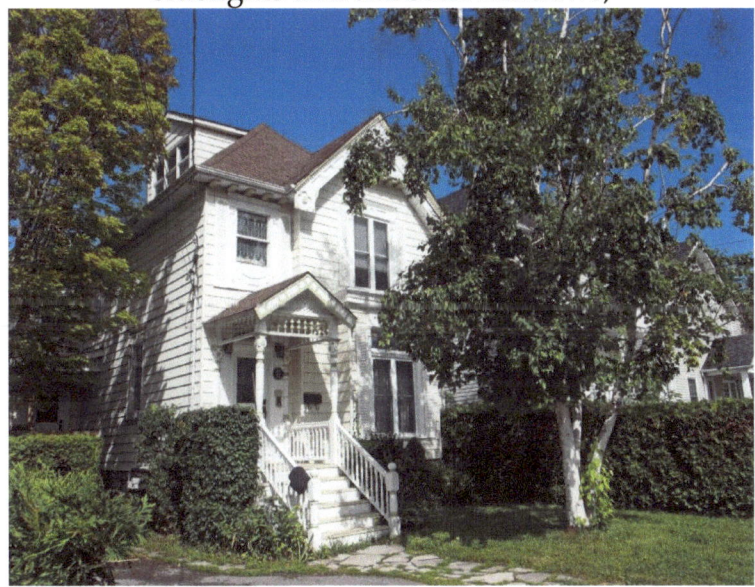

72 Pembroke Street – rectangular bay window, verge board trim on gable, dormer, spindles below gable of porch

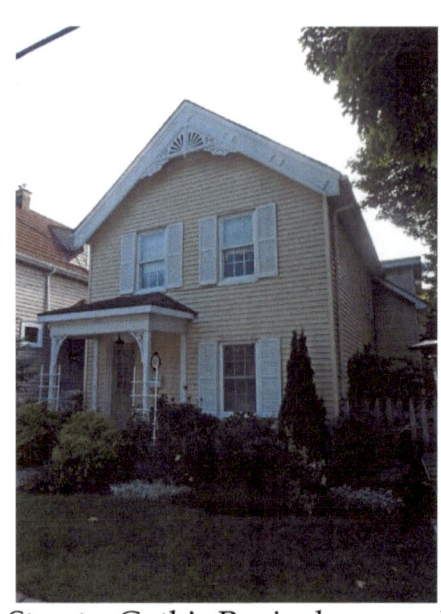

61 Pembroke Street – Gothic Revival – verge board trim on gable

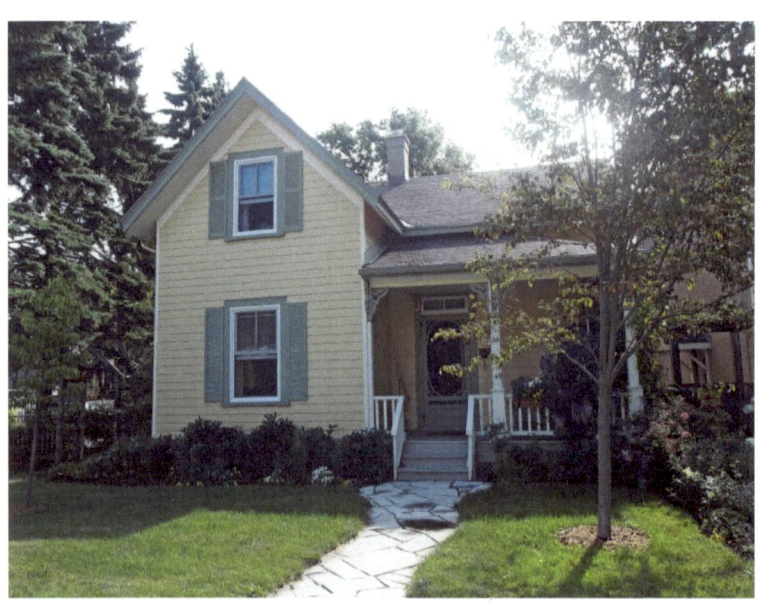

49 Pembroke Street

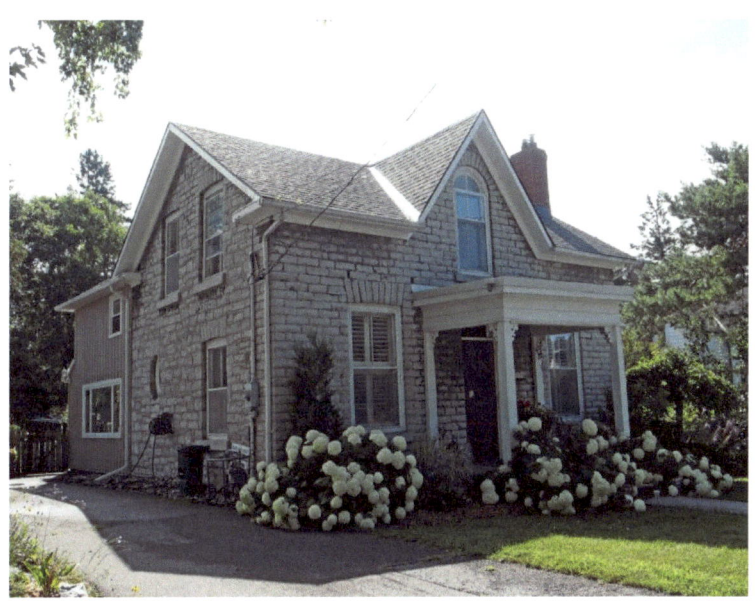

47 Pembroke Street – Gothic Revival, limestone, cornice return on end gables

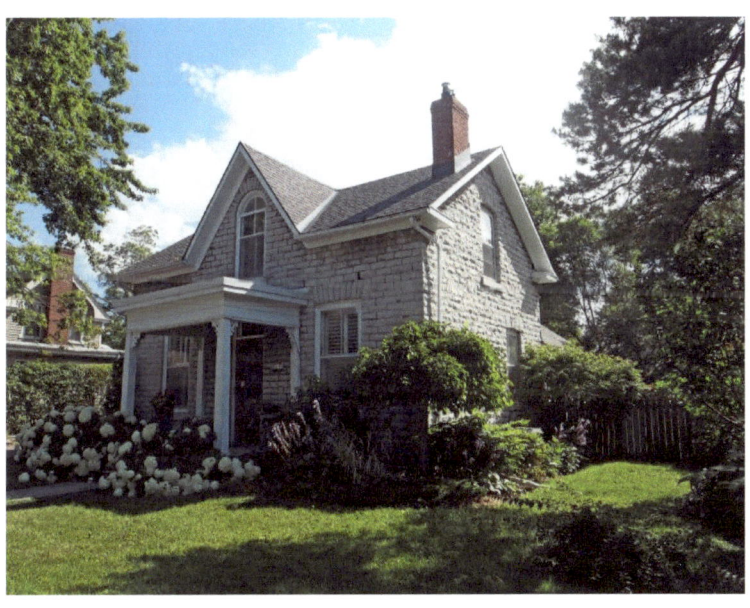

Bay Window: A window that projects out from a wall, in a semicircular, rectangular, or polygonal design. Used frequently in Gothic and Victorian designs. Example: 130 King Street East, Page 32	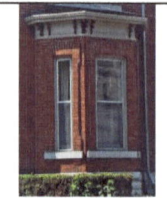
Brackets: a decorative or weight-bearing structural element which forms a right angle with one side against a wall and the other under a projecting surface such as an eave or roof. Example: 157 King Street East, Page 29	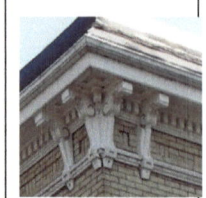
Capital: The uppermost finish or decoration on a column. An Ionic column has a small base, a thin elegant shaft, and a capital composed of volutes which are carved whirls or twists that take the form of a scroll. Example: 213 King Street East, Page 21 A Doric column is characterized by a plain column with no base, a shaft with twenty flutings, and a simple capital with a simple entablature. Example: 87 King Street East, Page 34 A Corinthian column is characterized by a rounded capital decorated with acanthus leaves and a square abacus (the uppermost portion of a capital directly below the entablature) on tall slender columns. Example: 149-151 Earl Street, Page 52	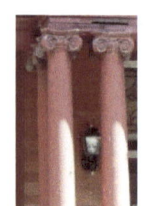 Ionic 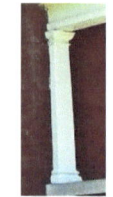 Doric 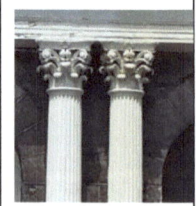 Corinthian

Cornice: originally the wooden overhang of the roof. With the use of stone, brick, iron and steel, the cornice is any projecting shelf at the top of a ceiling or roof. They can be very decorative. Example: 213 King Street East, Page 21	
Cornice Return: decorative element on the end of a gable. Example: Pembroke Street, Page 59	
Cupola: A domed or curved roof rising from a building as a decorative element. Example: 270 King Street East, Page 11	
Dentil Moulding: an even series of rectangles used as ornamental decoration in cornices. Example: 161 King Street East, Page 28	
Dichromatic brickwork: the use of two colours of brick, tile or slate to decorate a façade. Example: 320-322 King Street East, Page 8	

Dome: Any roof structure that is curved and spans an ultimately circular base. Squinches and **pendentives** are used to provide a circular base on a square or rectilinear tower. A squinch is a construction filling in the upper angles of a square room so as to form a base to receive an **octagonal** or **spherical dome**. When a square space is vaulted to provide a circular space for a **dome** the resulting curved triangular supports are called pendentives. This is most common in Byzantine architecture. Example: 270 King Street East, Page 11	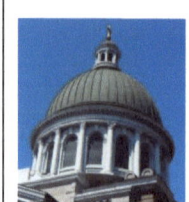
Dormer: (French for "sleep") a gable end window that pierces through the plane of a sloping roof surface to create usable space in the top floor or attic of a building by adding headroom. Example: 348 King Street East, Page 6	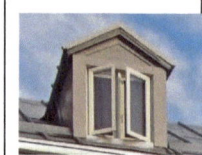
Entrance: The entrance encompasses the doorway and the inner vestibule or, in residential architecture, the covered porch. Example: 117 Earl Street, Page 50	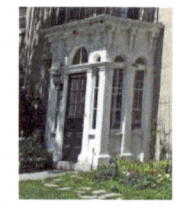
Frontispiece: a portion of the façade of a building, usually a centred doorway that is slightly raised from the rest of the building, usually has extensive ornamentation. Frontispieces are usually Classical in design with white columned porches. Example: 174 Earl Street, Page 56	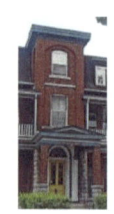

Gable: the triangular portion of a wall between the edges of a sloping roof. Example: 324-326 King Street East, Page 7	
Hipped Roof: a roof where all sides slope downwards to the walls with no gables. Example: 240 King Street East, Page 16	
Iron Cresting: A decorative ornament along the top of a roof. Iron cresting was popular in the Baroque era and also in Italianate, Victorian, Second Empire and Queen Anne styles of architecture. Example: 85 King Street East, Page 35	
Keystones and Voussoirs: a voussoir is a wedge-shaped element used in building an arch. A keystone is the central stone that locks all the stones into position, allowing the arch to bear weight. A keystone is often enlarged and embellished. Example: 126 Earl Street, Page 51	
Mansard Roof: This style was popularized by Francois Mansart (1598-1666), an accomplished architect of the French Baroque period and especially fashionable during the Second French Empire (1852-1870). This roof is almost flat on the top section, with two slopes on each of its sides with the lower slope at a steeper angle than the upper and having dormer windows. Example: 130 King Street East, Page 32	

Pediment: a triangular section above the horizontal structure (entablature), typically supported by columns. The inside of the triangle is called the tympanum. Example: 148 Earl Street, Page 52	
Pilaster: a slightly projecting column built into or applied to the face of a wall for additional structural support. Example: 328 King Street East, Page 7	
The **quatrefoil** is a type of decorative framework consisting of a symmetrical shape which forms the outline of four partially overlapping circles of the same diameter. The word quatrefoil comes from Latin and means "four leaves". Example: 212 Barrie Street, Page 57	
Quoin: masonry blocks at the corner of a wall, often a decorative feature, usually larger or of a different colour than the rest of the wall. Example: 169 King Street East, Page 26	
Rose Window: a circular window with ornamental tracery radiating from the centre. Example: 212 Barrie Street, Page 57	

Sidelight: a window, usually with a vertical emphasis, that flanks a door, and is often used to emphasize the importance of a primary entrance. **Transom Window:** the light above the doorway, also called a fanlight. Example: 28 Earl Street, Page 42	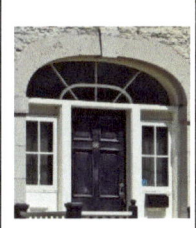
Turret: a small tower that projects from the wall of a building. Example: 95 King Street East, Page 33	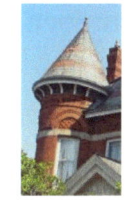
Verge board and Finial: also called bargeboards – hang from the projecting end of a roof and are often elaborately carved and ornamented. **Finial:** ornament added to the top of a gable, pinnacle, canopy or spire – a Gothic element. Example: 61 Pembroke Street, Page 60	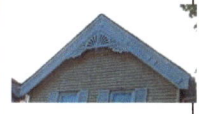
Window Hood: A **hood** is the piece found above window openings, usually of an ornate design, and covers the top third of the opening. Hoods are commonly placed above arched or curved openings on both windows and doors. Example: 169 King Street East, Page 26	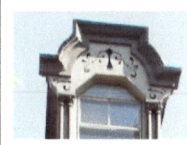

Classical Revival (1820 - 1860) – This style was an analytical, scientific, and dogmatic revival based on intensive studies of Greek and Roman buildings, concerned with the application of Greek plans and proportions to civic buildings. Schools, libraries, government offices, and most other civic buildings were built in the Classical Revival style. The white columned porches of the Classical Revival domestic buildings are identified with the mansions of wealthy land owners in Canada. Example: 294 King Street East, Page 12	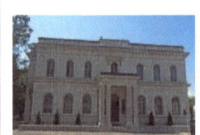
Georgian, before 1860 – This style began with the British King Georges in the 18th century. These buildings have balanced facades around a central door, medium-pitched gable roofs, and small paned windows. Example: 131-133 King Street East, Page 31	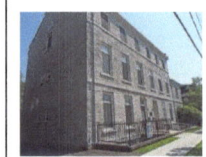
Gothic Revival, 1830-1890 – These decorative buildings have sharply-pitched gables with highly detailed verge boards, pointed-arch window openings, and dichromatic brickwork. It is a common style in Ontario. Example: 61 Pembroke Street, Page 60	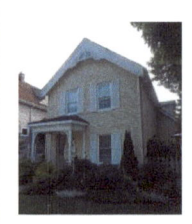
Italianate, 1850-1900 – It has wide-bracketed eaves, belvederes, wrap-around verandahs. Example: 87 King Street East, Page 34	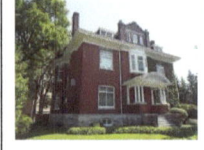

Neo-Classical (1810 - 1850) – This style was a direct result of the War of 1812. Many Upper Canadians returning from the war with the United States were second or third generation Loyalists who had inherited land and means from their forefathers. Once the conflict had passed, they had the money and the time to expand their holdings and indulge their architectural whims. Buildings were constructed on the traditional Georgian plan, with a new gaiety and light-heartedness with more refined, delicate, and elegant detailing. Example: 264 King Street East, Page 13	
Queen Anne, 1885-1900 – This style is distinguished by an irregular outline featuring a combination of an offset tower, broad gables, projecting two-storey bays, verandahs, multi-sloped roofs, and tall, decorative chimneys. A mixture of brick and wood is common. Windows often have one large single-paned bottom sash and small panes in the upper sash. Example: 95 King Street East, Page 33	
Victorian - In Ontario, a Victorian style building can be seen as any building built between 1840 and 1900 that doesn't fit into any of the other categories. It encompasses a large group of buildings constructed in brick, stone, and timber, using an eclectic mixture of Classical and Gothic motifs. Example: 157 King Street East, Page 29	
Tudor Revival – exposed timbers with stucco infill, multi-paned windows. Example: 81 King Street East, Page 36	

Renaissance Revival (1870 - 1910) - The Renaissance Palazzo was a three or four storey building with a rusticated (very large masonry blocks with deep joints and decorated with rough or bold finishes) ground floor, and regularized understated windows on two upper levels, finished by an elaborate cornice. In Ontario, the Renaissance was revived in commercial buildings, banks, offices, and churches in many towns. Most of the Renaissance Revival buildings are designed without columns while those with columns and pilasters are more ornate.

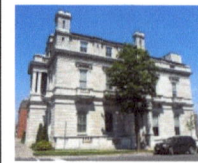

Example: 243 King Street East, Page 15

Romanesque Revival, 1880-1910 – This style hearkens back to medieval architecture of the 11th and 12th centuries with a heavy appearance, blocky towers and rounded arches.
Example: 212 Barrie Street, Page 57

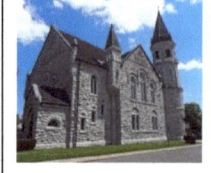

Second Empire, 1860-1880 – The mansard roof is the most noteworthy feature of this style and is evidence of the French origins. Projecting central towers and one or two-storey bays can also be present.
Example: 130 King Street East, Page 32

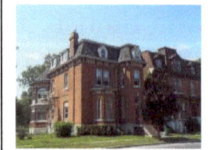

www.ingramcontent.com/pod-product-compliance
Lightning Source LLC
Chambersburg PA
CBHW040837180526
45159CB00001B/221